SAFEGUARD OUR FLANK

The Kensingtons

TERENCE KEAREY

SAFEGUARD OUR FLANK

The Kensingtons

MEMOIRS

Cirencester

Published by Memoirs

MEMOIRS
PUBLISHING

25 Market Place, Cirencester, Gloucestershire, GL7 2NX
info@memoirsbooks.co.uk www.memoirspublishing.com

Copyright ©Terence Kearey, August 2012

First published in England, July 2012

Book jacket design Ray Lipscombe

ISBN 978-1-909304-08-6

All rights reserved.

No part of this publication may be reproduced, stored in a retrieval system, or transmitted in any form or by any means, electronic, mechanical, photocopying, recording or otherwise without the prior permission of Memoirs.

Although the author and publisher have made every effort to ensure that the information in this book was correct when going to press, we do not assume and hereby disclaim any liability to any party for any loss, damage, or disruption caused by errors or omissions, whether such errors or omissions result from negligence, accident, or any other cause.
The views expressed in this book are purely the author's.

Printed in England

This book is dedicated to the memory of
Major A E Kearey DCM, one-time Regimental
Sergeant Major of the Kensingtons.

Now the day is over
Night is falling nigh
Shadows of the evening
Steal across the sky.

This Memoirs Book Presents a ninety-sixth Anniversary.

INTRODUCTION

When I was writing *History, Heroism and Home*, a historical overview of my paternal roots, I included my father's experiences during WWI. To do the subject justice I assembled the latest books, scoured second-hand bookshops and spent ages scanning the internet. They allowed me to pen a version that gave a travelogue through the war until the day my father returned home.

At the time, for what I was aiming at, this was sufficient. However, I resolved to write a fuller version of my father's Battalion's efforts at Gommecourt. This work is still not a definitive version, for which I apologise. It does however illustrate how difficult it is to get to the truth. My researches have exposed many false trails, dashed hopes and hidden facts; much lies buried with the participants.

I have now come to the conclusion that it is impossible to give a complete account, for even official documents do not carry the facts, nor do the individual Battalion records account for every event. Battles rarely go as planned, individuals are not automatons and the elements are contrary. These varying factors often defy the best-laid plans. So I have had to be content with getting a little nearer to the truth.

CHAPTER ONE

SHOWING THE FLAG

Since the end of the First World War there has been a continuing interest in all aspects of the conflict. Of all its battles, the Somme was probably the major event. Part of that battle's orders of the day was a diversion on the left flank at a place called Gommecourt. This French village and its environs held the Kern Redoubt, a fortified enclosure.

All villages bisected by the German front line were fortified. The houses were used as strong points, with gun emplacements and machine-gun nests. Their highest buildings – church towers and factories etc - were used for observation, mapping and sniping. Gommecourt, however, was slightly different from all the others, because it was the strongest.

The Kern Redoubt's strength was not obvious to the casual observer; it had reinforced cupolas for gun head cover and numerous concrete pill-boxes, like World War II beach emplacements. The position contented itself with deep trenches and dug-outs, underground troop positions and linking tunnels to rear areas, along with very thick barbed-wire entanglements.

You might think that if the place was known to be so

CHAPTER ONE

strongly fortified, perhaps a different approach from that which Lt-General Snow planned might have been adopted. That it wasn't could perhaps suggest bull-headedness, incompetence, even criminal negligence.

58-year-old Snow was the eldest son of the Reverend Snow of Langton Lodge. After attending Eton and Cambridge he obtained a commission in the 13th Regiment of Foot. In 1914 he received a wound at the Battle of the Marne when his horse rolled on him. He suffered from this injury for the rest of his life. A year after Gommecourt he was relieved of his post after a number of criticisms regarding his handling of the 7th Corps at both Gommecourt and Cambrai. After reading this account you might believe he was slighted, or, on the other hand let, off lightly.

A whole range of books have been written, historical, biographical and those given to commentary, or giving detail and substance to participating forces, weapons used and numbers killed. Most have given me pleasure to read and added to my store of knowledge.

My father, a one-time Regimental Sergeant Major, left a typewritten script which formed a basis to this study, but like most old soldiers he didn't go into detail. I have always been left wondering about the part he played.

Nearly a century on, many of the stories of that war are little known, particularly those involving offshoots to the main battle. Coming to the subject again I have been overwhelmed once more by what those poor men went through and what was expected of them. I shall do my best not to let them down in telling a more complete story of their suffering.

CHAPTER ONE

You might wonder how I could possibly better some offerings from the past. I can only reply that today there are more sources of information available to offer a fuller picture, and that I am motivated by an added personal interest.

I do apologise if I get a point wrong, miss out some outstanding event or omit a leading participant. However I make no apology for taking sides or engaging in hindsight. There have been songs sung, plays acted and stories written about the 'Lions and the Donkeys'. When you have read this you may wish to write or sing your own. The final series of the BBC comedy programme *Blackadder* had it about right. It is difficult to imagine men being ordered to behave in such a fashion, or accepting such balderdash from their superiors, but it happened.

Why did they not use their common sense when presented with such hopeless tasks? There is no point in attacking a trench which has barbed wire protecting it and it is clearly stupid to continue marching forward when men on both sides are being mown down.

Try as I might to find full lists of men taking part in the battle, I have failed. It is a pity that so many men have died without some mention, even a passing one. Officers are mentioned by name, deeds of valour given pride of place and trenches identified with familiar titles, while many cemeteries carry a message of the fallen. But who were the men who lived and continued to shoulder arms, and what did they do, those men who volunteered?

As with all British infantry Battalions, the Adjutant kept the day-to-day diary. He held the rank of Captain and was paid

CHAPTER ONE

the princely sum of 25 shillings a day for his labours. Unfortunately in war the post was often left vacant, leaving the onerous job to a junior ranker someone who was not so fussy in keeping the up-to-date detailed accounts.

For this book and my recording I have chosen what happened at the Battle of the Somme and its planned diversion 10 miles to its left, at Gommecourt. In particular I have focused on the part played by the Kensingtons, the guardians of its right flank at Hébuterne.

This was no flag-waving event of heart-wrenching valour. It entailed the extinction of over fifty percent of the Battalion's men in as many minutes. After the war, my grandmother wore black for the rest of her life, alternately wearing her four dead sons' medals every Sunday. Liddell Hart describes Armistice Day as a commemoration, not a celebration. Grandma had it about right, but it still led to another pointless war twenty years later.

The Kensingtons, a Territorial Battalion, lived and worked in suburban London. In the main they dwelt in the Borough of Kensington, between Notting Hill and Bayswater to its north and Chelsea to its south. Hammersmith lies to the west and Brompton to the east.

In the first quarter of the 20th century Kensington was noted, as it is today, for its royal gardens, its majestic palace and Imperial Institute. It was a place of Georgian villas and high street shops, a dormitory town for London's business class just outside the city. The closer you lived to Kensington Palace and the vicarage, the higher up the social ladder you stood.

The Kensington Regiment was adopted by the Royal

CHAPTER ONE

Borough in 1905, having been previously the 4th Middlesex. It retained its headquarters at Iverna Gardens, close to Bayswater Railway Station. The Battalion officers were in the main professional men working in the city. The men were made up of managers, self-employed craftsmen, clerks and railway workers. In the main the ranks were all well educated for the day, attending local board or church schools. They were not exceptional thinkers but they were as brave as lions, motivated by the opportunity for glory. They were kindred spirits, related to each other by school, street and expectation. Today we might call them a band of brothers; then they were called the 'Pals', all coming from a common place and sharing similar expectations.

Today we would question why so many men queued up to be taught how to kill and place themselves in a position of danger. There has always been the lure of the uniform and something compelling about marching behind the band and being 'one of the few.' Eventually, by training and association, each man would know his fellow as an oppo, a chum, squaddie or mate. Knowing these things, the politicians appealed to their binding power. Kitchener pointed his famous finger, declaring 'Your Country Needs You.' Having been given official recognition and authority, their chests swelled with pride. It gave each man a spring in his step as he prepared to march towards danger.

As the Kensingtons marched towards the front line they sang songs of the day and were united in body. They cemented their bonds and became a unit. Later, they didn't question what they were told, for they had volunteered to do as ordered. They wanted to be there to fight for king and country and to maintain the Empire. The few sceptics who joined the throng, not wishing

CHAPTER ONE

to be left out, sang with just as much vim and vigour as their mates.

When later they did form up on the trench parapet to march towards the enemy, they did so expecting to reach the German lines without being fired at, for they had been told that no man's land would be a walkover. That it was nothing of the kind came as a big surprise. Perhaps it was self-delusion that made most believe what they were told, or unthinking optimism; perhaps loyalty to the corps or regiment, who really knows?

This band of volunteers had its beginnings handed down from ancient feudal rights, regulated by sheriffs, shire and hundred courts. The geld and fyrd was a means the king and parliament used to gather together an army. This was not the only body of amateurs the king relied upon. County militia systems trained citizens between 16 and 65 in the use of guns, armour and horses in case of need.

The Volunteers were formed in 1778, ostensibly to fight the French. It became popular for young men enrolling in the mid 19th century to bear the expense of their equipment and uniforms, paying an annual subscription of five shillings.

This organised and conforming body of men naturally went down very well with the Government, which saw it as a means whereby they could call on trained men. The local authorities could see that this would give cause and place for the active young, to keep them off the streets. As for the ladies, it is said they preferred men with a spring in their step, a military bearing and in uniform. At any rate it gave the men something to do and kept them out of the public houses. Joining the Volunteers became the 'done thing' and particular regiments could pick and chose their recruits. The Kensingtons

CHAPTER ONE

were one such regiment, filled with eager, well-motivated and keen young men just raring to 'have a go'.

Thirty years before, the Lords Ranelagh and Truro had agreed to dress their men in a uniform of grey, with red facings and a glazed peak shako. Black belts were buffed, trimmings of buff laces dressed and silver appointments polished, all the height of fashion for the well-dressed military. Not long afterwards, the Boer War changed all that and the British military establishment elected for khaki in the field.

As the Kensingtons marched through Le Havre their steps echoed on the narrow, cobbled streets. Some 29 officers and 835 men, in small pack order, strode along at 120 paces a minute. They had set out that cold November day to march to Watford and from there to take the train to Southampton, eventually to form up on the dockside to cheers from the French residents.

The Battalion suffered its first casualties on November 19th and they quickly became accustomed to the realities of the front line. They spent their first Christmas standing in trenches knee-deep in water.

An attack was planned in company with the French at Vimy to take Aubers Ridge, which turned out to be a very costly move. The fighting was so severe that the Battalion lost half of those men who had set out so confidently in November. They amalgamated with the London Rangers, who had also lost fifty percent of their number. When replacements became available from training Battalions in England both Battalions reformed, taking back their own identities. For most of that year the Kensingtons operated in lines of communication, unloading supplies at railheads.

CHAPTER ONE

By late spring the following year, both the Kensingtons and London Rangers were in training. They were attached to the 56th Division of the 168th Brigade. This gave the replacements time to become familiar with the old salts to make the Battalion a unified whole once again.

Vigorous training schedules were the order of the day, to enable them to become proficient with the new Lewis gun, Stokes mortar and Mills bomb. Lectures were given about the new German flame-thrower, the gas attacks and how best to use the respirators to resist its worst effects.

Steadily, as each company became proficient, they took over the Hébuterne 'Y' and 'W' Sectors positioned on the left of the Somme front. The village lay opposite Gommecourt, astride the D27 and D28 roads.

During and after the battle of Loos, Sir John French was thought to be 'out of tune with his Army.' This was the thinking of General Sir Douglas Haig, who believed the Commander in Chief had allowed a chance to make a major break in the German line to slip away. Haig undermined the senior man's position by casting doubts about his tactics. It worked and French was retired. The unfortunate Sir Ian Hamilton, who was the next senior officer and much more experienced, was bypassed.

Gallipoli had not gone well. It had been dogged by the Navy's unpreparedness. This allowed Haig to step into the vacant position created by Sir John French, who retired on 19th December 1915.

General Joffre wished to retain control of the Allied Forces. To ensure this would happen he placed the French Sixth Army

CHAPTER ONE

alongside the new British Fourth Army under its commander, Lieutenant General Sir Henry Rawlinson.

Haig had an army that had been enlarged from four divisions in August 1914 to 58 two years later. To support this number it was necessary to have a comparable infrastructure. Haig's headquarters was well behind the front line. His commanders, each with his own headquarters, was a further distance away, so communications between commanders and their troops was difficult to maintain particularly during a battle.

Once battle had been initiated, steady, reliable information from the leading troops was impossible. Once the battle plan had been agreed and put into action, there was nothing left to be done but continue with it, even if there were in some instances overwhelming reasons to change it.

The pre-battle artillery bombardment ordered by General Rawlinson was so intense that most telephone lines were cut even though they had been laid six feet under the ground, or two feet below the duckboards in the trenches. During the battle some important messages were not answered for more than five hours, in instances where the artillery had to change its firing pattern or a communication trench had to alter its use. Discretion suggested they should be left alone.

A communication trench runs at right angles to the firing line, linking it to the rear. They are used to give cover and access to the troops manning the front line and passing the rear for replacements. They provide cover for caterers, weapon supply, runners and medical orderlies.

The area commander directs that one communication trench

CHAPTER ONE

is for 'up' traffic, to the front, while the other is for 'down' traffic, to the rear.

Messages, unless clear and simple, can be a distraction; some have been known to cause total confusion during battle. This problem was recognised by General Rawlinson, whose doubtfulness about the Territorial Army's efficiency added to his insistence that the 'Big Push' was to be won by sticking to the plan and by rigid training by rote, taking away any on-the-spot decisions.

There is no doubt that the orders issued by the British GHQ before the battle were comprehensive. But were they the right ones and who, at the front, was to see that they were carried out or changed to take account of developments?

General Haig, was a cavalry man. The job of battle commander was that of General Rawlinson, an infantryman who had just returned from Gallipoli. He had been appointed by Sir John French, now retired. Rawlinson distrusted the quality, resourcefulness and tenor of the Territorial Army. It was in his nature to be dogmatic, insisting on attrition by his guns rather than surprise and preferring a rigid wave formation to adopting the natural contours of the battlefield to give shelter and access. His artillery was expected to win the battle and all other aspects were left to tactics set down in detail and comprehensively written up in 'orders of the day', which everyone had to keep to.

Communications on the battlefield before and after the start of an attack were primitive and extremely unreliable. On the order to move forward the infantry was thereafter lost to strategic command. The generals had no idea what was

CHAPTER ONE

happening: how successful the artillery was, how efficient the smoke-screen or whether the first wave had progressed. It was not known if the timing was kept to, what casualties had been inflicted or if the follow-up plan was taking account of what had gone before.

The Somme offensive was the result of the Chantilly Conference attended by the Allied commanders on December 5th, 1915. General Joseph Jacques Césaire Joffre, aged 62, was the Allied Commander in Chief. He believed that the autumn offensives in Champagne and Artois had been tactical successes, only brought up short by bad weather and lack of ammunition.

Prior to the Somme the Battle of Loos had been undertaken by the 47th London and 15th Scottish Divisions. They had done all that had been expected of them by taking the mining village of Loos. It was then necessary for reserve divisions to be thrust in to strengthen the line. This was not achieved, and Sir John French paid the price.

In early 1916, battles were fought and pressure mounted across the whole northern front. These were planned and executed to take the pressure off the French troops at Verdun, where the German Crown Prince's army had pushed the French back. The main British contribution was to be enacted on The Somme, a battle which was described as The Big Push.

Lt-General Allenby, the British Third Army Commander and Lt-General Snow, its VII Corps Commander, devised a plan for the diversionary attack on Gommecourt and had it delivered to General Headquarters on the 4th June 1916. Snow was given the task of pinching out the Gommecourt salient

CHAPTER ONE

which stuck out on the Fourth Army's left flank. It was hoped that this would be sufficient diversion to draw German attention away from the main attack up the main road to Bapaume. The troops allotted to Lt General Snow were the 46th North Midland Division and the 56th London Division, plus detachments of Engineers and Pioneers.

This story is about the part played by the London Scottish and in particular their support Battalion, the Kensingtons. Major General Hull, the 56th Commander, instructed the Kensingtons' Colonel Young to 'safeguard our flank'. This was to be achieved by digging a connecting trench across no Man's land and manning it. This special task was given to Major Cedric Dickens, Young's second in command.

Cedric Dickens was Charles Dickens' grandson. He was a dedicated Territorial who had attended Eton and Trinity Hall and had trained as a solicitor. He was well known and liked, playing a central role in the Battalion. His men were in the main office workers and businessmen. It needed someone of Cedric's standing to be respected and followed.

The Territorial Army was an updated version of the Volunteers, who were part-time soldiers paid an hourly rate, exactly the same amount as the regulars. They attended an evening's drill session once a week, shooting at weekends and undertaking a fortnight's summer camp every year.
This force was raised to defend the country while the regular troops were abroad.

Their headquarters and drill halls were built in most large towns, with their members drawn from the local citizenry. They were not expected to serve overseas nor transfer to other units

CHAPTER ONE

but in fact they did. It was these men, together with the Regulars, which made up the British Expeditionary Force. They became known as the Terriers and were considered to be part of the nation's social fabric. The gentlemen were the officers and the players were the men.

If this sounds rather amateurish and light hearted, in many respects it was. It could be described as a club where local men met, acted out a soldier's life and had a drink at the bar. Most regiments and Battalions had their own masonic lodge, which was a further binding institution. Every so often there was a dance, an annual camp, or an outing for the officers and their wives. Weekend shooting at various ranges, including Bisley, was a respected pastime in the Battalion's calendar.

The sergeants too had their club and bar, as did the men. This volunteer system allowed the government to have a body of men who worked together, were immediately on hand for an emergency and understood military procedures.

The Volunteer reserves were and are an important fabric of the country. Having them in place allowed the government to use them for emergency relief and to back up the police force and other national services. The regular officers were in the main men of the middle classes, conservative in persuasion, although ignorant of political theory. Their pursuits were hunting, playing cricket and after-dinner games, often involving horseplay. Talking shop was 'just not done'. As Alun Chalfont remarks in *Montgomery of Alamein*, 'The BEF was an army almost totally irrelevant to the needs of the situation'.

Five years before war broke out it was obvious to all that Germany was increasing its armed forces to a degree which

CHAPTER ONE

took it beyond home defence or national security. It became apparent that the German aristocracy and military leaders were flexing their muscles and that a small incident could explode and turn into war, and this is exactly what happened. Belgium's neutrality was violated, King Albert's appeal to King George was met and Imperial Britain found itself at war.

Now the Territorials were needed. Men who had trained on the heath and were led by the nation's professional classes were called to the colours. These men became controlled by an officer class whose previous experience was based on the African Wars, where Churchill had ridden in the last cavalry charge at Omdurman. This was a force not long out of their scarlet uniforms.

Throughout the war, neither side really achieved a breakthrough. The last Allied push, which came right at the end of the war in 1918, succeeded only through America's intervention with men and equipment. The introduction of tried and tested massed tank formations did finally reap its just reward. The battle on the Somme was fought right in the middle of the conflict. You will see how desperate the struggle was and how futile the sacrifices which were made.

There are two accepted methods of defeating a strongly held position. You can break through the enemy crust and push out into the country beyond, then circle back and pinch out the enemy's supplies, or inflict repeated hammer blows, smashing all before your outward surge. Both need intelligence and information, but the former needs hands-on direction from the front.

CHAPTER TWO

STRATEGY AND TACTICS

In 1916 the British and French Headquarter staff and their respective political leaders came to a joint agreement: their countries' soldiers were at a disadvantage. The German Imperial Army was better trained, better led and had better weapons. All this enabled them to hold their western front and consolidate, while looking ahead for the next conquest.

This recognition of Germany's strength was seen not just in France but on all other fronts too. Russia was finding it difficult to sustain its effort, while in the Dardanelles Hamilton had called off the unequal struggle. Serbia was crushed and the Italians were reliant upon the munitions of its allies. Closer to home at Ypres the combined western forces had been held at bay and Kitchener had died at sea. There was little to give light and hope.

This was reflected in the differing attitudes between the two sides. The Germans were in the main defending their gains, quite content to sit it out and wear down the attackers, whereas the Allies were always pressing, attempting to get behind the opposing front line. The former's philosophy was to dig deep and establish their position. The latter wanted to be on the move and not become bogged down.

CHAPTER TWO

The Chief of Allied Command, General Joffre, was of the opinion that success could be achieved on the western front. As the French Supreme Leader he authorised the reduction of the French overseas forces. This would give him more men to build up his depleted forces. He had been led to believe that the Russians would build up their army during the winter and would do their bit when the time came for a spring offensive. There was concord at the British and French headquarters. Spring was to bring glad tidings.

When possible the Germans had always chosen the high ground. Not being pressed for territory, they would make a step backwards to achieve this. Now General Haig was being pressured not only to relieve Verdun but to prepare a better jumping-off place for future operations. He nominated General Rawlinson to command his Fourth Army. If detailed planning held the key to winning battles, this was going to be a walkover.

General Rawlinson intended to make it his business to produce a plan of operations that was second to none in detail. Field Marshal Kitchener became Minister of War; he had no illusions that this was going to be over quickly or cheaply, in material or manpower.

By 1915 it became clear that more troops were needed, and a plan was put in place to recruit 500,000 more. At the same time normal recruitment was continued in Regular and Territorial units. 'Your country needs you!' was the adopted slogan. It was Kitchener's magnetism that galvanized the youth of the country to join the ranks.

By the end of that year, 2.2 million men had volunteered. Many of them were in France, about to fight at the Battle of

CHAPTER TWO

Ancre. During the interim period, training took place. Selected officers, NCOs and men were detailed off for front-line experience, attached to serving units.

When major attacks were to be fought a core of each Battalion was generally kept aside to train any new intakes should disaster befall. This was a sensible move and paid off later after the Somme battles, when so many men were lost.

The training consisted of maintaining a number of set routines. Before dawn the men were roused to prepare for 'stand to' and 'man the fire steps'. This was to prevent a surprise dawn raid. On many mornings there were the usual 'hate' first shots, made to inform the enemy that you were alert and on guard.

Men cooked their own breakfasts in small groups, shaving, washing and cleaning. In between duties they continued fetching and storing supplies. Both sides were doing exactly the same thing and respecting each others' periods of domestic calm. At night the reverse occurred, until all was relatively quiet. Then the night owls came out to repair the wire, lay signalling wire, repair trenches and parapets and be detailed off for working parties. Sentries were posted and patrols sent out to capture prisoners, survey the ground ahead and arrange the laying of trip wires.

At French Headquarters, Pétain was promoted to command the Tenth Army Group and Nivelle given command of Verdun. On the 11th of June Pétain asked Joffre to speed up the British attack. He was desperate because Fort Vaux had fallen and he needed relief from German pressure.

Twelve days later the Germans introduced the diphosgene

CHAPTER TWO

gas shell, and panic set in. It paralyzed the French artillery. Three days later the Germans almost scaled Belleville Heights, the last outpost of Verdun. Pétain made ready to evacuate the east bank. Four divisions were quickly dispatched by Joffre, further weakening Rawlinson's force.

The French were facing huge losses of a hundred thousand men per month. They needed a strategic diversion, and only the British Army could provide it. Joffre and Haig agreed that the British Fourth Army would attack along a fourteen-mile front north of the River Somme, preceded by an artillery bombardment lasting five days. The French Sixth Army would attack on a six-mile front south of the river. It was this army which became whittled down as troops were withdrawn to bolster up those at Verdun.

General Haig's opinion was that Guillemont was not the most suitable place to make a breach in the German line. Nor did he concur with General Rawlinson's preference for a sustained artillery bombardment followed by an orderly follow-up by waves of infantry. These tactics he allowed to be followed only under a certain amount of duress.

Rawlinson was an infantry General and Haig a cavalry man who was new to the job. When Haig accepted the entreaties by General Joffre to give succour to the French troops at Verdun, he relied upon Rawlinson to deliver the goods.

General Haig was a man of supreme confidence in his own self-worth. This self-opinionated man was one of many such leaders. Perhaps they had gained their high opinions of themselves by fighting armies from nations which were inferior in both military thinking and hardware. Headquarters staff

CHAPTER TWO

considered that as military leaders from the world's greatest Empire, they were naturally superior. This confidence in their ability was misplaced. Their military skills proved to be sadly lacking.

The British Army's General Headquarters staff were as good as any and the planners second to none. What was lacking was good infantry tactics.

General Rawlinson's tactic, used during the earlier stages of trench warfare, was to shell the enemy front line, allowing the British infantry to advance and seize the front. However, his tactic of preliminary sustained bombardment was largely unsuccessful.

The nature of no man's land, filled with barbed wire and other obstructions, was a factor that had to be taken into consideration. For a British unit to get to an enemy trench line it had to cross no man's land, secure the enemy position, then face counter-attack. It also depended on the ability of friendly artillery to suppress the enemy, and this was frequently thwarted by the Germans' deep dugouts and revetments. The British suffered from not having suitable ammunition and by their artillery's inaccurate fire. No attention was paid to the infantry having freedom of movement, making use of the terrain, operating covering rifle fire and night fighting.

In Haig's second Despatch, printed 29th December 1916, he submitted the principle of the Somme battle. It draws attention to his army's lack of training that any attack had to work in unison with what the French, the Italians and the Russians were doing, while laying great emphasis on the pre-battle preparations regarding military and human necessity. He

CHAPTER TWO

went to great lengths about the difficulties he had been faced with, claiming rightly that the German front and rear lines had been strong and that flanking fire from both machine guns and artillery was going to be a problem.

The report is copious and lengthy, going into great detail on relatively minor excursions. The proof of a battle's worth must be to compare the final casualty figures and the psychological effects it had on both the armies. Strong, well-planned night attacks along the whole front line, made by area commanders knowing their front intimately, would have created the same relief to the French as to the British and saved many thousands of men's lives. However, I digress; you will have to make up your own mind.

The assault on Verdun by the German Crown Prince Rupprecht of Bavaria created confusion. If matters got out of hand for the French the offensive might turn out to be a totally British responsibility, and that was something the French definitely did not want.

Rawlinson returned to his headquarters after accepting that the French Sixth Army was going to join in the general assault. He gave orders that all the corps commanders, heads of staff and the various branches should meet up. This included Generals Hunter-Weston, Morland and Congreve, as well as Birch, the chief gunner, and Montgomery, Rawlinson's chief of staff.

Rawlinson laid out a detailed report of his findings. The army would attack in June or July. VII Corps would join them from the Third Army. The artillery would be reinforced by heavy howitzers and there would be no stinting on ammunition expended.

CHAPTER TWO

There were to be many batteries to back up the big guns. Actually there were not that many guns at the time; the numbers were doubled later.

A new order from headquarters required signalling cable to be buried at least six feet into the ground. Complex switch lines were to be laid and roads reinforced, with some widened, and the railway track was to be extended to get closer to the front line.

Considering the poor weather and over use, the trenches had to be repaired and where possible deepened. All this extra administration and supply needed a reserve of 4000-5000 men to keep pace. These front-line maintenance programmes and improvements were led and organized by the engineers.

The strength of the Fourth Army and the GHQ Reserve would double the numbers of men to 500,000, with 100,000 horses and an increase in motorized vehicles. Training was put in hand immediately so that every part of the battle plan was understood. General Rawlinson laid great emphasis on the necessary supply of oil and fuel, water and foodstuffs. Dugouts were prepared for the medical centres, dressings and drugs stocked up.

By the end of 1915, after the Battle of Loos, the front quietened down. It was obvious to all that although many men had died, the end was still nowhere in sight. At home the country was at last waking up to the terrible conclusion that this was going to have to be outright war and everyone was going to have to contribute. Only new tactics, weapons and attitudes were going to win through. Gradually, as more men were enlisted and taken from the workplace, women took

CHAPTER TWO

over their jobs. In many instances they did them better. Women proved more amenable and capable of more intricate work where precision was required.

The Kensingtons needed replacements to make up their numbers. After receiving another batch of reinforcements from England, they were back up to strength. A new training schedule was devised to make the Division ready for front line fighting. This was neither the first time the Battalion was reinforced nor, as it turned out, the last.

The reformed brigade marched off to Loos station and there entrained for Pont Remy. Arriving in pouring rain, the brigade marched off again to Citerne. This village, set in undulating countryside with few cottages or hamlets, was rural in the extreme.

The weather was squally with occasional heavy falls of snow. Again, the brigade was housed in bell tents in a muddy field. The next day they engaged in strenuous training exercises using the latest tactics and weapons.

The automatic Lewis gun with its pan of bullets was going to be an improvement, so too the new grenades and Stokes mortar. Every day groups were detailed off to become expert in the use of these weapons, while wearing the new-style gas masks. Route and speed marches, in full fighting order, were made at least once a week; distances over twenty-five miles soon led to men dropping out, to be picked up later by wagon. At last the division set off away from Citerne to Longpré, a large farm complex.

By the time the Battalion got to Longpré many men were complaining about blisters. They had short shrift from the

CHAPTER TWO

sergeants, who told them that it was an offence to have blisters and if there were any more complaints the malingerers would receive punishment for not taking due care. This soon settled everyone down. Guards were detailed off and the rest collapsed, utterly exhausted. There were no blankets or food until the following day.

The roads were congested by marching Frenchmen and wheeled artillery, all racing to get to Verdun. Their movement delayed the Battalion from continuing, so they had a couple of days of forced rest, interspersed with whatever practices the sergeants could think up to keep them occupied.

The rolling hills and shallow valleys gave Picardy the appearance of Salisbury Plain. Compared to Ypres it had space, unobstructed views and open countryside, suitable for unrestricted action. Those of a more frivolous nature described it as good hunting country. Below ground were layers of chalk, ideal for constructing deep shelters and communicating trenches.

The Germans were experts at making the most of their front line, putting all their ingenuity into making substantial living accommodation to back up the forward troops. Both sides dug like mad to make extensive trench systems. Once again, the object was to take the strain off the French, who were suffering many casualties at Verdun.

It is well to remember how the land north of the Somme was defended and by whom. In September 1914, both the Germans and French tried to outflank each other until the British laid claim to the Channel ports, the French the Pas de Calais, the Belgians an area of land west of the river Yser and the Germans the industrial heart and the coalfield of Belgium and northern France.

CHAPTER TWO

In February 1916, when Joffre intended to offer up an offensive riposte to areas north and south of the Somme, he passed over the French Tenth Army's front to the British. By spring 1916, Allenby's Third Army held the land to the north of Hébuterne and the Fourth Army land to the south; this area of combat was changed after the second day of the battle to call The Reserve Army. The Fourth Army Sector was concentrated further south – on Bécourt.

The French had been the temporary custodians of Foncquevillers and Hébuterne. This was French land and they wanted the invaders out. The British wanted to get the war over and return home, but the French wanted their usurped land back. Both wanted movement, not static defence. The Germans had taken the land, its resources and industry and had for the moment other fish to fry – they were also fighting the Italians and the Russians and were not in a hurry to move. They thought they might as well make the station comfortable and secure.

The German command had to instil discipline and order to make their men happy. They set the men to work to make the line impregnable, letting the local commanders devise the best ways to make their front efficient and militarily daunting to the enemy.

There is no better way for a leader to get cooperation from the men than to give them a chance to make their life more comfortable. The German trenches were in many cases fifteen feet deep, with dormitories, cook-houses, latrines and wash areas, stores and armouries, all cut or buried into the ground, boarded and propped. There were stairs, companionways,

CHAPTER TWO

with reinforced head covers, wattle and board trench sides and raised duckboards. Gun positions, machine gun nests, trench mortar pits, pill boxes, sentry boxes, observation and periscope sites were all frequently constructed using concrete.

The trench system was linked to communication trenches running back to their rear lines, with tunnels leading to vital sectors, many lit by electricity and the sides taking telephone wires. Isolated hamlets, villages and factories, bisected by the front line, adapted and converted into fortified positions as forts along the wall.

The German artillery and machine guns were laid and registered on to key British positions, with the distances indicated by marker stakes. This preparation allowed for immediate firing; each gun was capable of overlapping lanes of fire with their next along the trench to cover the open ground ahead and where possible enfilade on either flank. All along the front banks of staked barbed wire, many yards thick, ran out into no man's land.

It was these well-constructed trenches that the first wave, then the second, had to suppress, navigate and pass through, allowing the third wave to clear by bombing and taking prisoners. Further waves brought along spare ammunition and grenades and later ones got down into the trenches to reverse the firing steps and open up access points and clear blocked intersections and shell damage. Finally the stretcher-bearers attended to the wounded and the dead. All this had to be negotiated and made secure before a breakout could attack the enemy rear.

During early May the 46th Division was out of line, resting

CHAPTER TWO

in their billet at Lucheux. After the mud, cold and wet of Vimy, they appreciated the better weather, the good billets and the excellent country in which they now found themselves. The Château de Lucheux and the gateway stand on the edge of a forest a few miles north of Doullens. As in all out-of-line camps fatigues were carried on; in this case, the men made revetments to line trench sides.

The 56th Division marched to Souastre, continuing their training much as the 46th were doing at Lucheux. A fortnight later they set off again to march to Hébuterne, while the 46th occupied their billets at Foncquevillers. Both these villages held old French lines prepared in 1914. The sixteen or so miles both Divisions had to make were completed in the morning. Divisional Headquarters allowed them two days' rest exploring their local villages, doing some washing and having canvas baths.

Shouldering their rifles, they formed up again to march on to Magnicourt. There they continued practising attacks and had further instruction of bombing and another exhibition of the German flamethrower, being told its uses and problems. The Generals were continually thinking of ways to keep the men occupied to prevent boredom and slack ways.

The Germans had launched a massive attack on the French Line at Verdun on 21st February 1916 and the battle was still raging; the French had lost almost half a million men. To alleviate the strain on the French it was decided that the British should make a strong attack on the Somme. Although the battle has been given the name of Somme it was in fact the Battle of Ancre, another river more central to the action.

CHAPTER TWO

This battle was not planned in isolation. The policy was to keep pressing the Germans on all fronts in unison, which included the Italian and Russian fronts. All units had to send in night attacks to take prisoners and extract information about the opposing formations. The main battle front lay between Gommecourt to the north and Maricourt in the south. On the north of Ancre lay the village of Beaumont Hamel and Serre four miles south of Gommecourt.

The administrative department of Somme takes its name from the river which runs through the region. The part held by the British was the northeast corner, overlapping into the next department, the Pas de Calais. This region of France formed part of the old province of Picardy; an old Roman road linked its cathedral city, Amiens and two smaller towns of Albert, northeast of Amiens, and further still Bapaume.

The region was crossed by the Somme and the smaller Ancre. The Germans were defending their gains, the Allies intent upon pushing them back. The former constructed deep secure trenches and dugouts while developing small villages into miniature forts. The latter believed such tactics created a 'sit it out' attitude. The British high command trusted to mobility and attack.

The Germans always seemed to hold the high ground; not only could they observe what was going on, but they knew that any attack had to be made uphill. They were more interested in securing a defensible position than gaining more land. If this suggests that their leaders were more able, militaristic and forward thinking, perhaps they were. What was true is that they were on somebody else's land and their

CHAPTER TWO

supplies came by road, not by sea. As the advantage in war always favours the attackers, the Germans held the stronger position.

Both sides were at this time depending on attrition – pounding their opponents into the ground. Not very subtle, but the victor would be he who could sustain it longest. Putting in attacks that held no chance of being sustained or were designed to end the campaign was wasteful. The battle of the Somme is a case in point. It was never envisaged that it would finish the war and it certainly never had sufficient resources. The result was stalemate. Both sides were soaked in blood and worn out, for it all had to be gone through again. Did the powers that be ever learn any lessons? I am not sure they did. The age of the tank and American intervention was to come.

CHAPTER THREE

A DIVERSIONARY MOVEMENT

When General Haig planned this battle he wondered how he could give the attack a better chance. While he considered this, he told the commanders of his First, Second and Third Armies to carry out constant threatening moves to keep the German troops on their toes. Like all good commanders he consulted his intelligence section and took soundings from his staff.

He came up with a diversionary movement. This was not a new idea, as all commanders do this - placing a movement at a distance from the main attack, the flanks being ideal. On Haig's left was a salient sticking out of the German line. This was a continuing sore which would be the perfect place. Gommecourt, for that was the name of the salient, would be ideal. As he could not take any forces away from General Rawlinson, Haig contacted General Allenby, Commander of his Third Army, to request a Corps transfer. Allenby chose the VII, which contained the 46th and 56th Territorial Divisions.

Their task was to mount a full-scale attack on Gommecourt. The object was to remove the salient if possible, but more importantly to cause a diversion to stop German reinforcements backing up their troops opposite the main

CHAPTER THREE

British thrust, which was to be an advance up the main road from Albert towards Bapaume. This main force was Lt-General Rawlinson's Fourth Army, backed up and supported by Lt-General Gough's Reserve Army, which was hoping to break out into the country beyond.

Neither Allenby nor Rawlinson liked the plan, because there was a gap between their Army and Rawlinson's Fourth, leaving no protection to the right flank of the attacking force between Gommecourt and Serre, the preserves of Hunter Western's X Corps.

Behind Gommecourt to the north was the Quadrilateral, a defensive position surrounded by tracks. Southwest lay the village: the high street, crossroads, château, park, wood, orchards and cemetery. By the time of the battle there were three lines of German trenches and interlocking communication trenches, plus their dugouts and fortified posts. The whole lot constituted the Kern Redoubt.

From the centre of the main British attack at Albert, Gommecourt is some ten miles to the north. All the villages through which the German front line ran were turned into fortified strong-points. The Kern Redoubt was one of them, if not the main one, and as such it was going to be an extremely hard nut to crack. This was not obvious to the casual observer, for all the main troop locations were underground with passageways leading to specific locations and key outer defences.

The machine-gun nests were camouflaged, some with top cover, others in strategic positions dictated by the attackers' approach. The German defending artillery was used for

CHAPTER THREE

counter-battery and bombardment and was hidden by a number of woods. In front of the firing line was staked barbed wire, strung to a minimum depth of ten feet. Both the 'Little Z', a ziz-zag on the eastern flank, and the 'Z' just before the village, a finger of parkland jutting out on the centre, allowed machine gun fire to enfilade the Sherwoods attacking the wood.

Lieutenant General Sir Thomas D'Oyly Snow KCB, KCMG, 1858-1940, was born in Newton Valence, Hampshire. He attended Eton and St John's College, Oxford, obtaining a commission in 1879. Promoted Captain 1887, he took part in the wars in Africa, reaching staff rank in 1897. At the outbreak of the First World War he commanded the 4th Division, finally becoming commander of the VII Corps on 15th July 1915. His force at Gommecourt comprised the 46th North Midland and 56th London Divisions.

It was Snow's plan, and his alone, to create a pincer movement around the strongly-held Gommecourt Park, the tip of the German salient. He had, however, no freedom of action about the numbers of artillery pieces he could muster, the type, the numbers of shells allowed for each gun or the timing of his attack. For these he had to conform to the main battle plan devised by his senior commander, General Rawlinson.

The diversion's main aim was to draw German attention away from the main battle area and keep them occupied, whereas Snow's plan smacks of a 'positive aggressive action' to encircle, crush and take. If he had planned a single push using all his forces on the weakest part of the German front line – somewhere where they could not be shot at by machine-gun fire, while making his flanks secure - his action would

CHAPTER THREE

have had a far greater effect. A narrow front allowed a greater concentration of fire on batteries on the front and in the rear.

The then current General Staff instructions were that no attack should be made which involved having to advance more than 200 yards towards the enemy. Snow stressed before the battle to his two divisional commanders: 'This is a diversion to support the main battle, your role is a strictly limited one. There are no reserves and your attack should only take place when the German defences have been destroyed by the artillery'. These limiting factors were restrictive and important guidelines. They indicate that there was no strategic point in the attack and that success depended on a single outcome – the occupation of the German trenches. During the attack all Rawlinson's limiters would need verification checked by a trustworthy officer, who would then report back. Presumably General Rawlinson received this.

There are no references to an on-the-spot examination, nor to who was to make the decision or by what means the information was to be carried back to those in charge. Only the commanding officer at the front could decide if the German defences had been destroyed sufficiently to be sure any attack would be successful. If he could not be certain by personal knowledge he would need good, reliable information passed to him. On the day, neither of these conditions were met. Within the first few minutes it was clear that the German defences had not been destroyed, and within two hours it was clear that here there was a disaster in the making.

Opposing his men, General Fritz von Below's 2nd Guards Reserve Infantry Division (III Corps, 15,000 strong), was

CHAPTER THREE

formed in August 1914 from non-Guards reservists from Westphalia, Hanover and smaller German states adjoining Prussian provinces. They included artillery, cavalry and engineers. The Division was made up of the 26th Reserve Infantry Brigade 15th & 55th Regiments, and the 38th Reserve Infantry Brigade, containing the 77th & 91st Regiments.

From spring until late June 1916, there was feverish activity along the whole Allied front which was gaining momentum. It was obvious to all, particularly the Germans, that there was going to be an attack. This was even more evident to the German 2nd Reserve Division Reserve Regiments; all were purposely allowed to see British preparation taking place. This was part of the ruse to draw attention away from the main British attack.

General Haig's plan was to create a series of feints along the whole front and to make them obvious. This order was carried out to the letter and all preparations were made openly. In May, von Below was informed by his Operations Branch that air surveys had reported the construction of a broad-gauge railway, new highways and gun positions. Falkenhayn ordered his pioneers to construct a third line of defence to give extra retiring positions.

A detachment of 8" howitzers was transferred, made up of captured Russian guns. However, Falkenhayn believed the British would only pin down the front, not make a serious attempt at Gommecourt. However, by 1st June, Below worked out by evidence that the British were going to attack Gommecourt and he ordered his men to be watchful. Practices were carried out to see how long it would take from a warning

CHAPTER THREE

to get men up from the deep dugouts, assemble their machine guns and start firing. The eventual target was three minutes.

Fritz von Below and Prince Rupprecht were right in expecting that the Gommecourt Salient would be one of the main targets. Falkenhayn thought the British attack would be further north and refused to send extra troops. At the start of the battle the Germans were outnumbered seven to one. Lt-General Snow told General Haig, 'They know we're coming all right'. Von Below reinforced the Gommecourt Sector with the 2nd Guard Reserve in the middle of June and later with the 170th Reserve Regiment.

The 2nd Guards Reserve Division, part of General Stein's 14th Reserve Corps, was commanded by General Freiherr von Susskind. The German savours of the salient were the 15th, 55th, 77th and 170th Regiments. All these German units had, at full strength, a composite of 800 men in each of nine Battalions. This was approximately half that of the British. The main difference between the two armies was in training, the number of machine guns, artillery support and provision of appropriate ammunition. Originally there were two German regiments and their artillery holding the salient. This was increased to four, with a number in support. The two new regiments brought with them their artillery to add to the 19th and 20th Reserve Field Artillery Regiment's fifty-plus which were already positioned there. A number of heavy howitzer batteries were included. All these guns could reach the VII and VIII Corps troops stationed opposite Serre, Beaumont Hamel and Gommecourt.

Behind the 56th Division was the beautiful village of

CHAPTER THREE

Hébuterne. The capital of the area was Amiens, where the cathedral declared the region's religious obedience. The land was described as chalkland. Hébuterne was one of the area's largest towns. A few cottages lined the road, with tall, stately trees, behind which lay orchards and gardens. Among these trees the French had constructed a number of trenches. The place was typical of the region. All the buildings were built of red brick except the church, which was of imported stone.

The main employer in the village had been the owner of the brick-built mill. Its ruins and cellars now formed the Battalion headquarters, with all the usual staff: adjutant, RSM, clerks, runners, signallers and cooks etc. The entrances were protected by sandbagged abutments. The French had also constructed trenches on the eastern side of the village, closest to Gommecourt Wood, using a number of interconnecting communication trenches to give access for supply teams during the hours of darkness. Nearby was a bunker known as the Keep.

The village nestled between the British 3rd and 4th Armies, opposite the salient village of Gommecourt with its château, park, wood, a famous tree - the Kaiser Oak - and crossroads. In parts of the front line, the German trenches were only fifty feet away with a hedge in between. The Germans could be heard talking to each other.

By the time the British occupied their front line in 1916 Hébuterne was a ghost town, a shadow of its former past, for it was already in ruins. Yet though the village and church had suffered terribly the tower still stood proudly silhouetted against the sky. As with all points of interest the Germans had

CHAPTER THREE

the church entrance well within their artillery range and zeroed in. Even though the entrance had been sandbagged it was a dangerous place to linger. If you stand at the Hébuterne crossroads looking a mile north, you see the village of Gommecourt with its cemetery and park. Between Hébuterne and Gommecourt grew a hedge, interspersed with a few trees which lay in a coombe, a slight valley at an angle to the rise. This is where an advance trench was to be prepared.

The attack at the Gommecourt salient was to be a diversionary one to delay or stop German reinforcements backing-up their troops in front of the main British attack up the supply route from Albert to Bapaume.. It was to be made by the main British thrust up the road, the main supply route from Albert towards Bapaume. This Big Push was to be made by the British Fourth Army led by General Rawlinson, backed up and supported by the Reserve Army of Sir Herbert Gough, who, it was hoped, would exploit the penetration by creating a rout in the German rear.

Gommecourt is on a slight rise, dominating the countryside around. The trees in the park had been stripped of their foliage by shellfire, making the place ghostly, as if possessed by evil. The village, park and cemetery were within the Kern Redoubt and its administration centre was the Quadrilateral, a fortified box formed by tracks on all sides.

The German front-line trench outlined the geographical spur and the village complex. Behind the line ran the D6 from Foncquevillers south to Serre. The coombe between the two chalk banks was no man's land. The crucifix on the British front line stood on the shoulder of the valley.

As with all German-held villages on their front line, the

CHAPTER THREE

buildings became fortified strong-points, making this a very strong fortified position. In front of the German trench line ran barbed wire strung on iron stakes in a series of rows, the wire making the position impregnable. The trench was serviced with support and guard lines all linked to the communication trenches stretching back to the central fortress.

The German front line was a deep trench, well revetted and bearing a parapet. It was dug twelve to fifteen feet deep and shored up at intervals with timbering and wickerwork. Along its length it was further strengthened by reinforced bomb-proof shelters. Cut into the rear of the trench were deep dugouts, some with their own periscopes on tripods. It was the job of the observation squads to inform their colleagues if an attack was being made.

A number of tunnels and cuttings led back to the new third trench, and one in particular led back from the Z on the D6 to the Staffordshires' front, which was to make such an important contribution to the German counter attack.

When the alarm was raised by the German observers, their shout triggered a three-minute timed response. Their machine-gun teams assembled their weapons for rapid fire. It was these machine-gun teams and supporting artillery that were the chief danger to both advancing Divisions. They were placed where they would do most damage, having a clear field of fire and each situated where they could enfilade the area to their front.

The German artillery parks, of all calibres, were hidden in the woods behind Gommecourt. They were equal, if not superior, in number to their British counterparts. Forming the hub of all this was the command centre at the Quadrilateral.

CHAPTER THREE

The whole salient formed a dent in the British Sector. The Germans had the time and the inclination to make themselves as comfortable and as impregnable as possible.

The German 170th Reserve defending this fort wanted to survive and see another day. Part of the German defence was to set up their machine guns so that they could sweep their front and cross over to cover the next gun's field of fire along the line. At night each gun was set up on fixed lines to cover a particular weak spot or gap in the wire. The gun could be discharged at irregular moments throughout the night, dissuading nightly patrols and capture and repair parties.

Against the Germans were pitted the 46th and 56th Divisions. They were going to be asked to walk across no man's land in line, evenly spaced out and trying not to bunch up or take shelter. If they could keep pace with the advancing barrage, they were assured that the Germans were not going to stand up on their firing steps but would keep their heads down. This creeping barrage was there to force the enemy to keep below their parapet.

As there had been almost continuous gunfire for the previous week to destroy the banks of staked barbed wire and gun nests, taking the Redoubt was not going to present a problem – or at least this was the considered belief at British Headquarters. Others who were less knowledgeable thought it was going to be a walk over.

Two days before the attack, patrols reported that there were great gaps in the German wire and some of the German positions had been vacated. On the 46th Division's front, patrols reported there were no gaps and that there was a large unreported hollow in the ground that was filled with half buried wire.

CHAPTER THREE

The weather was squally, with occasional heavy falls of snow. Again, the brigade was housed in bell tents in a muddy field. The next day they engaged in strenuous training exercises using the latest tactics and weapons. The automatic Lewis gun with its pan of bullets was going to be an improvement, as were the new grenades.

Every day groups were detailed off to become expert in the use of these weapons, including the use of them while wearing the new style gas masks. Route and forced marches, in full fighting kit, were made at least once a week and were over twenty-five miles in length. They soon led to men dropping out, to be picked up by wagon. At last, the Division set off away from Citerne to Longpré.

In October 1915 the Battalion casualties had been so bad that the Kensingtons and Irish Rangers had amalgamated. Over three months in early 1916, when replacements became available from training Battalions in Britain, they were shipped over to fill up the places, allowing both Battalions to reform. Both were now in training at Halloy, which gave the replacement troops time to become familiar with the old salts and for them all to become proficient with the new Lewis machine gun and Stokes mortar. Particular emphasis was laid on their bayoneting skills. Lectures and demonstrations were laid on to reintroduce the skills necessary. Steadily, as each company became proficient, they took over the Hébuterne sector, on the left of the Somme front opposite Gommecourt.

CHAPTER FOUR

FACE YOUR FRONT

A close study of the Somme battles and particularly the attack at Gommecourt, although a subsidiary, gives a picture of the thinking processes of those engaged in organizing and conducting warfare at that time. A great deal of confidence was shown towards what was expected by the various artillery pieces and their ammunition. Here is a list of effects the guns were expected to deliver:

- Destroy the will of the opposing forces.
- Kill as many of the enemy as possible.
- Lay waste to enemy dugouts, underground bunkers and guard posts.
- Destroy their counter batteries, artillery and rear facilities.
- Stop supplies from getting forward.
- Produce chaos in the enemy's rear.
- Break up the staked and coiled barbed wire.
- Lay down a smoke-screen.
- Fire ahead of advancing troops.
- Destroy, when necessary, identified gun-sites and machine-gun nests.

CHAPTER FOUR

Time and again in both world wars it was proved that artillery did not achieve what was expected, even with great care in sighting and laying the guns. It needs a spotter's identification to register a correct fall of shot before trying another, and even then you do not know the actual result.

To fire a gun half a mile away from the target so that the shot falls into a trench three feet wide needs many attempts. The shell must be fused to ensure it explodes before being buried in the mud, or just at the lip of the trench to achieve maximum devastation.

It is a great challenge to take out a machine-gun nest built three sandbags high to give cover to the height of a crouching man sitting on the ground in a five-foot wide pit. The trench had to be large enough to accommodate his number two, spare ammunition and cooling tank, and covered with a shrapnel-proof roof of turf which protected and camouflaged the nest.

The Germans were purposely forewarned about the attack, but not the timing. At the start of the barrage they had either dropped below the parapet into a twelve foot deep dugout or retired back to a rear trench. They had practised many times to get to their weapon pits, erect their guns and stand to in three minutes.

Staked banks of coiled barbed wire, even when subjected to exploding shrapnel, is not always severed and even if it is, it doesn't just fall to the ground in neat pieces but resumes its coil – it tends to spring back. To rely upon it being passable when so much was at stake, with no proper verification, was foolhardy.

CHAPTER FOUR

Until the following year, when more tanks appeared, the wire would continue to be one of the great hazards for the battle planners. As soon as the enemy saw that an effort was actively being made to cut, blow up or tow away their wire, they knew an attack was imminent.

General Rawlinson's 'Wave System' involved an advance behind a rolling barrage. This creeping barrage was laid down a hundred yards in front of the leading wave – usually 'A' Company of the advancing Battalion. They would fall in on the trench parapet and face the enemy. Each man was to be positioned five yards apart, a hundred yards between waves, with their arms at the port. Their advance was to be slow and deliberate, no faster than two miles per hour. To ensure they maintained the correct distance behind the barrage, there was to be no stopping for any reason. The Battalion would take nine minutes to pass a given point and cover an area 400 x 900 yards.

It is obvious that any enemy machine gun still operating would create havoc to such slow-moving lines of men, as it did for the Sherwood Forester's first waves advancing towards the Quadrilateral; likewise the German artillery barrage from behind Serre, ranging in on the Kensingtons, who were about to dig the communication trench to their front in no man's land.

WEAPONRY
THE RIFLE

The troops engaged in the attack on the Kern Redoubt were mainly infantry. The basic weapon in 1916 was the SMLE (Short

CHAPTER FOUR

Magazine Lee Enfield) Mark III, made by the Enfield Manufacturing Co Ltd. First produced in 1903, it was designed by the American James Lee and built at the Royal Small Arms Factory in Enfield. It had a 10-bullet magazine and a high rate of fire. Much has been written about its quality in comparison with the German Mauser. The fact that the same design was used for over fifty years of manufacture speaks for itself as to its usefulness and reliability. It was a most excellent rifle and served the Country and Commonwealth with distinction, being capable of operating at over twenty rounds a minute. The short Lee Enfield went out of use during the Malayan War in 1948-1960.

SIDEARMS

The Webley revolver at the outbreak of the First World War was the Mk V, adopted December 1913. On 24 May 1915, the Webley Mk VI was adopted as the standard sidearm for British troops and it remained so for the duration of the First World War, being issued to officers, airmen, naval crews, boarding parties, trench raiders, machine-gun teams and tank crews. The Mk VI proved to be a very reliable and hardy weapon, well suited to the mud and adverse conditions of trench warfare.

VICKERS MARK I MACHINE GUN

A development of the Maxim gun had been in service with the British Army since the turn of the 19th century. The gun was water-cooled and fed by a canvas belt holding 250 rounds. The gun was served by a team of nine, usually an officer, two

CHAPTER FOUR

NCOs and six other ranks. All ranks were expected to take each others' jobs in an emergency. During the attack on the Redoubt a number of these guns were taken over and used against the German lines. Their use was mainly restricted to protecting the right flank or when men were falling back when the attack petered out. Any other firings had the possibility of becoming friendly fire.

LEWIS LIGHT MACHINE GUN

Once again this was a weapon devised in the USA, in 1911. It was air-cooled with a rotating magazine fitted on the top. It was lighter, cheaper and simpler to manufacture and became the standard British close-support automatic weapon.

MILLS GRENADE

This was a hand-held bomb, invented in 1915 by William Mills. It was a hand-thrown cast iron fragmentation bomb with delayed action fuse, weighing 1.5 lbs with a firing lever release pin. It had a 30-yard range and a 10-yard killing zone. Bombing parties were formed to clear a trench, its traverse and mined dugouts. In normal fighting the Mills grenade was used for house and pill-box clearances.

STOKES MORTAR

Sir William Scott-Stokes, a civil engineer by trade, was Chairman and Managing Director of Ransomes & Rapier of

CHAPTER FOUR

Ipswich. He invented the trench mortar in 1914 and it was made ready to use at Loos firing smoke canisters. It used a cartridge fired by a raised pin and could be adapted to fire fragmentation and solid shot up to 800 yards. Over time, after many modifications, it became extremely versatile, simple to use, quickly set up and very portable.

BANGALORE TORPEDO

This torpedo was the only way to effectively clear a path in barbed-wire defences. The tube could be loaded with gun cotton or dynamite sticks and several lengths of tube could be joined together, depending on the width of the barbed wine entanglement. The firing element comprised a fuse and safety pin which set off the charge in tandem. The object was to thread the tube through the wire, not push it along the ground. It was the job of the Royal Engineer detachments to make those breaks in the wire.

The final bombardment started at 0600 on the 1st July. The gunners had saved up for this occasion. It was the greatest bombardment which had ever been laid on and it went on all along the front. The ferocity lasted an hour before the leading formations rose up out of their trenches. The ground shook. Earth crumbled and split apart and cascaded down the sides of the trenches; it was a terrifying, teeth-clenching experience. Fountains of mud, dust, smoke and débris shot into the air. Anyone brave or stupid enough to look over the parapet would be staring into Dante's Inferno and hearing the crump,

CHAPTER FOUR

whistle, whine and shriek of metal fragments whizzing through the air.

The British gunners did try to focus their weapons on particular targets, but they were as inexperienced at their task as the infantry were at theirs. They were certainly not the highly-trained men of the French School of applied artillery and engineering in Fontainebleau. Great attention was paid to bombarding known strong points in the park, the centre of the village and the maze of trenches the London Scottish were going to pass through, along with Nameless Farm and the little and large Z points in the line that could enfilade the 46th Division's advance. Further north was Pigeon Farm, another German strong point.

The Infantry saw the gunners' jobs as to take out the opposition's guns and destroy his barbed-wire; this is what they had been told by their officers.

The field siege guns and howitzers were under the command of Brigadier General C M Ross-Johnson, Royal Artillery. The heavy artillery was controlled by Brigadier General C R Buckle and the Chief Engineer was Brigadier General J A Tanner. These leaders believed they could do all that was asked of them. The British guns at the Somme fired some 20,000 tons of various-sized shells, a total of 1,627,824 individual shells, according to the Official History, but they were the wrong sort of shell. It requires high explosive to damage trenches and the British did not have enough. Three-quarters of all the shells fired were shrapnel, useless for affecting anything that was well covered or for cutting barbed wire.

CHAPTER FOUR

Mud, and there was a lot of it on the front, absorbed and cushioned the metal particles. The harder the surface the more effective the fragmentation when the shell explodes, whatever the type of shell. A great many shells were dud or did not explode. Their effectiveness was reliant upon perfect manufacture of the explosive charge, the correct amount of explosive material placed in every shell and the weight of each shot being precisely the same.

The gun had to be stable, with its trailing bars firmly anchored and mounted on solid ground. The bore of the gun must not be worn and the sighting arrangement had to be secure. None of these essentials made any difference until the sighting shots, straddles (one shot over and one under), were plotted and registered accurately.

This early in the war the Army was still operating on a pre-war mind-set. Such things as conveyor-belt manufacturing, chemical composition, ballistics, distances, angles, mathematics and mapping points were not greatly studied by the regulars, let alone the Territorial units. Intelligence gathering, ciphers, information sifting, gun emplacement recognition, photographic evidence, sound location and aerial spotting were primitive.

The communication methods were largely ineffectual, especially once the battle had begun, though they were necessary for accurate gun laying, firing, observation and achieving scored hits working under the command of forward observation posts in contact with the advancing troops.

Indirect fire could be done off the map, but the maps used in France were not good and at the start of the war they were

CHAPTER FOUR

not squared or gridded. Various other methods were used, adopting aiming posts or triangulation. Fire was corrected by observation, because the battery observer and target were not accurately fixed. Errors in range were not very significant due to the range zone of the gun, but errors in line meant always missing the target.

The Royal Flying Corps was commanded by a former Lieutenant-Colonel of the Royal Scots Fusiliers, H M Trenchard. The RFC had two categories: spotting for the artillery, photography and reconnaissance; and bombing and fighting in the air.

Before and during the battles which encapsulated the battle of the Somme, close cooperation between the Flying Corps and the gunners was paramount. Special flights were made that involved artillery observation specifically to reduce the opposing guns. The relatively new craft of air photography became an exact science.

Bombing too began to be taken seriously and became highly organised; night flights for particular targets, those greatly defended by small arms, became a serious occupation. Number 43 Squadron was the first long-range strategic reconnaissance squadron engaged in assessing military build up in the enemy rear.

CHAPTER FIVE

THE NORTHERN SECTOR

The first action the 46th North Midland Division was engaged in was at the Battle of Loos, when they attacked the Hohenzollern Redoubt. This was another of the strongly-held fortified villages along the front. The 46th had been the first territorial Division to land in France and it was by the Lancashire Fusiliers that they had been instructed in the art of trench warfare.

On 1st June 1914, Major General Wortley (1857-1934), became commander of the British 46th North Midland Division. The Division was part of General Allenby's Third Army. On 20th April 1916 the Division was withdrawn from Vimy and ordered south. By May it was at Lucheux, recuperating after the battle's horrors. The 46th Division was billeted in Foncquevillers and commanded by Major General Hon. E J Montagu-Stuart-Wortley. They were attached to Lt-General D'Oyly Snow's VII Corps. His Corps was part of the Third Army, whose General Office Commanding was Gen Allenby. The Division incorporated the North Midland Division, which was to attack the north side of the fortified village of Gommecourt on the left flank on the British Line.

CHAPTER FIVE

The Division was made up of three brigades: the 137th, led by Brig-Gen H B Williams, which included The North and South Staffordshires; the 139th, commanded by Brig-Gen C T Shipley's 1st, 5th, 6th, 7th and 8th Battalion Sherwood Foresters, and in support, the 138th Brigades, 1st, 4th and 5th Lincolnshires, led by Brig-Gen G C Kemp. Last but not least were the 1/1st Monmouthshire Pioneers, who attended to all the field engineering work.

As the Division began to gather together at Lucheux they were ordered to practise their bayoneting while providing a variety of servicing and communication skills - building pipelines, laying track and building roads, trenches and gun pits in preparation for the Big Push. They were now attached to General Rawlinson's Fourth Army. Their task was to help liberate the Gommecourt salient by linking up with the 56th coming towards them from the other side of Gommecourt Park.

While the Staffs and Sherwoods had been practising for the attack on the 1st July the Lincoln and Leicestershire Battalions were occupying the British Front Line before Gommecourt Park and Wood. There on the 4th June they patrolled at night and improved the conditions in the trench, which was suffering under the continuous downpours of rain. While they were there they were told they were to be attached to the 46th Division.

It was during the practices simulating the attack on Gommecourt that the Battalion commanders came to the conclusion that they could not manage all that they were being asked to do. They appealed to General Snow and he agreed to loan them the Lincoln and Leicester Battalions, which were to provide three companies from each to line up behind the Staffordshires and Sherwood Foresters, bearing extra stores and ammunition. The fourth company was to dig a communication trench stretching from the British front line to the German one across no man's land, to aid supply and keep men acting as reserves safe from shelling.

On the 24th June the British artillery started to zero in on the German guns to the rear of Gommecourt, hidden in Pigeon, Biez, Square and Rossignol Woods. These shots were meant to zero the guns on to the targets. Unfortunately it requires accurate bracketing shots to be sure that when the time comes those targets will be hit. The gun barrels and rifling have to be new, the shells have to fit accurately and have exactly the same amount of propellant, the gun trail has to be properly secured and the ground under the wheels firm.

The Observation Sections, whose job it was to register the fall of shot, were responsible for maps, flash spotting and sound ranging. Considering all these factors you would not want to rely upon the artillery taking out the opposing guns. Unfortunately that is exactly what General Rawlinson did. It was only the previous October that counter-battery work had been left to the heavy artillery and a special officer, with the necessary assistants, had been attached to each Group Commander. By July 1916 the system was still in its infancy.

Surveyors were organized into Field Survey Companies RE, one per army. Each army had an observation section for flash spotting and a sound ranging section. At the battle of the Somme information was passed via telephone exchanges. These, however, were frequently destroyed.

CHAPTER FIVE

On the night of the 27th June, the area suffered 48 hours of continual rain. The Staffords and Sherwoods filed into the forward trench early the next morning, where they tramped knee-deep in mud and slime. The battlefield before them was a quagmire, with shell holes filled with water. It was a most depressing sight. It was obvious that the attack would flounder, especially as the men had to carry such a vast amount of extra material.

At the last minute the attack was put back 48 hours, to the 1st July. Now the men in the front-line trenches had to be withdrawn to allow them to dry out and rest. The Sherwoods and Staffords had to return to Lucheux to demonstrate a practice run to General Snow before they returned to perform the real thing.

At 0624 on the 1st July the final shells were sent over using high explosive and smoke. Trench mortars provided more accurate distribution of smoke bombs. Few doubted the Germans had been destroyed, so the bombardment had been a moral boost. At 0727 the Sherwood Foresters discharged the final rounds of smoke into no man's land.

At 0730 the Staffordshires and Sherwood Foresters climbed out of their new forward trench using ladders or steps cut into the trench sides. Their sergeants helped to pull the men out under the watchful eyes of the Captain and his Lieutenants, who would themselves fall in behind their own companies, with the Company Runner and Engineer/Signaller next to the Captain. All the 'A' Companies of each Battalion would line up on their parapet dressing, five yards between each man. They would advance side by side until they had covered one

CHAPTER FIVE

hundred yards. The first three waves would total 600-700 men.

The day was bright and clear. They moved off at a steady pace with their rifles at the port, bayonets in the air. Behind them further waves lined up and followed them. There was no shouting or light banter; they were all too nervous, wondering what was going to happen to them. The sergeants, as much to bolster their own courage as anything else, told them to keep in line and not bunch up, but the ground was pitted with holes half full of water and there was no way they could keep a perfect line.

The Sherwoods passed over the German front line and disappeared into the wood. When the time came the 'B' Companies would climb out and do the same thing, each company Battalion and supporting Battalion following one behind the other and keeping to a steady two miles per hour so that the artillery bombardment put on to keep the German heads down would be a hundred yards in front of the first wave.

Each man was carrying his battle order kit, a spare pair of socks and extra ammunition. Later waves would bring forward duckboards to span the German trenches, ladders to reach down to the bottom, spare ammunition and grenades and digging tools. So far everything was going well. The first two waves had got across and there was no reply from the enemy. They were soon lost from sight.

Suddenly they felt the wind freshen. It sent a shiver down the spine as the smoke swirled about and then began to clear. Now the whole panorama presented itself to the German observers.

The attack by the 46th went as follows:

The 17th Sherwood Foresters, commanded by Lt-Col Hind,

CHAPTER FIVE

were to capture the German trenches and the Food and Fork trench to their front, leaving later waves to clear up and reverse the firing step. They were to push on past the Schwalben Nest to the Quadrilateral, there to link up with the 1/9th London Rifles, Queen Victoria's.

The 1/6th Sherwood Foresters were split into two: two Companies were to back up the advancing 1/5th and two the 1/7th Sherwood Foresters. They were all to clear and consolidate the captured trenches.

The 1/5th Sherwood Foresters, commanded by Lt-Col Wilson, were to advance and take the German front line, make their way through Gommecourt Wood and head for the Quadrilateral to give support to the 1/7th.

The 1/8th Sherwood Foresters were to act as a reserve formation, bringing supplies up to the front and looking after the spare ammunition and grenades while collecting up the wounded.

The 1/5th North Staffords, commanded by Lt-Col Burnett, were to form extra waves following behind the 1/6th North Staffords too clear German trenches and bear supplies into Gommecourt village and Park.

The 1/6th North Staffordshires, commanded by Lt-Col Boote, were to take the German front line and move quickly into the village to support the 1/6th South Staffords in taking the Keep, a strongly fortified position, and meet up with the London Rifles coming from the south.

The 1/5th South Staffords, commanded by Lt-Col Raymer, were to form extra waves following behind the 1/6th South Staffords to clear German trenches and bear supplies into Gommecourt village and Park.

CHAPTER FIVE

The 1/6th South Staffords, commanded by Lt-Col Thursfield, were to split, one half meeting up with the 1/4 London Rifles and the other taking the German Fist trench guarding the Park, bypassing the Kaiser Oak, to attack the rear of the Germans in their front line trench Fit and Fig.

The 1/4th Lincolns Regiment were commanded by Lt-Col Barrell. Three Companies were to form an extra wave behind the 2 1/6th Companies of the Sherwood Foresters, acting as carriers to supply spare ammunition and grenades and to tidy up and clear the German trenches. 'D' Company were to dig a communication trench across no man's land, to ease the supply chain.

The 1/5th Lincolns Regiment, commanded by Colonel Sandall, were to send three Companies to form an extra wave behind the two Companies of the 1/6th Sherwood Foresters. They were to act as carriers to supply spare ammunition and grenades and to tidy up and clear the German trenches. The final Company were to dig a communication trench across no man's land, to make safe the supply chain.

Lieutenant Colonel W H Young assumed command of the Kensington Battalion on the 28th June 1916, just two days before the attack at Gommecourt. Major Cedric Dickens, the second in command, had been with the Battalion since entering France and had a far greater understanding of the officers and men.

The 56th London Division was probably the most highly trained territorial division in the British Army. Its four component parts had seen a lot of action already, losing few men but maintaining a high proportion of their original pre-war

CHAPTER FIVE

volunteers. The men were in the main well educated, working as managers and office workers in London's business sector.

The Kensingtons formed part of the 56th London Division in January 1916, after the war office authorised their reformation. By the end of the following month the Division's composition was complete, being joined by the 1st Battalion Cheshire Regiment as their Pioneers and the 1st Field Ambulance Section ready for the battle of the Somme.

Major-General Hull based his plans for the attack on Gommecourt on orders given to him by General Snow. Snow conformed to decisions made by Lt-General Rawlinson, who was in overall command. Snow's brief was to create a diversion at the salient to draw German attention away from the main battle area. He was also told there were no reserves and no troops set aside to take advantage of any gains made.

General Snow, conceding that the German defences were strong, decided to plan an encircling movement to attack from the flanks. Concern about the distance between the two front lines led to a plan being put into effect to dig two new trenches in no man's land before both Divisions' sectors.

On the 56th Division's front the task was given to Brigadier-General Loch. When the trench had been completed, his orders were to keep it occupied with his 167th Brigade, which was made up of two Battalions of Royal Fusiliers and two of the Middlesex, until the attacking troops took over prior to the battle.

Hull was in command of the 56th 1st London Division, and the attached pioneer Battalion, the 1st Cheshires, occupied the British sector south of Gommecourt. This was the right arm of

CHAPTER FIVE

the pincer movement surrounding the park and village. They were to meet up with the 46th North Midland Division coming towards them from the north side, led by Major General Wortley.

According to Brigade orders, Part II, 'Success is assured and casualties are expected to be 10%' (Martin Middlebrook's *The First Day on the Somme*). This assumption that the mission could not fail was handed down from General Headquarters and was widely believed by all senior commanders. Their confidence was misplaced, but it dominated every facet of the battle's planning.

The reader will become aware that the orders of battle – the tasks set for the 46th and 56th Division - were almost identical, there being just one or two changes to do with their positions on the battlefield that were different. In effect, their orders were the same. They were facing the same enemy, using the same tactics and would be using the same weapons. The distances were approximately the same too, as indeed was the goal.

The 56th London Division, commanded by Major General C P A Hull, included the 167th Brigade, made up by the 1st Royal Fusiliers, the 7th Middlesex, the 3rd Royal Fusiliers and the 8th Middlesex. The 168th Brigade, commanded by Brigadier-General Loch with Brigade Major Captain Neame and Staff Captain Major Wheatley, had as their Battalions the 4th Royal Fusiliers, the 13th Kensingtons, commanded by Lt-Col. Young, the 12th London Rangers and the 14th London Scottish. The 169th Brigade contained the 2nd Royal Fusiliers, the 9th Queen Victoria Rifles, the 5th London Rifles and finally the 16th Queen's Westminsters. As their Field Engineers they had the 5th Cheshire Pioneers, commanded by Lt. Col. Groves.

CHAPTER FIVE

Major General Hull's plan was for the 1st London Rifle Battalion Royal Fusiliers, commanded by Lt. Col. Wheatley, to advance at Zero Hour from Y48 trench, take the German Fen and Ferret trenches, pass on to take Female trench and bear left at the Cemetery, setting up two strong points either end. They were split: one section to enter the park, take the Germans in the rear, then set up a strong point at the southern edge of the park, while another would to meet up with the Staffordshires and a third would head for the village to meet up with the remaining Staffords.

The 1st Queen Victoria Rifles, commanded by Col. Dickins, were to advance from Y49 trench, take the German Fern and Fever trenches, pass on to take Feed and Flint, continue over to secure the German rear trench and set up a strong point at the junction with the communication trench Epte.

The 1st London Rangers, commanded by Col. Bayliffe, were to advance from Sector W50 trench, take the German Fetter and Fate trenches, pass on to take Felt trench and Nameless Farm, secure the German rear trench and set up a strong point to enfilade the ground beyond, at the bend in Fame.

The 1st London Scottish, commanded by Lt. Col. Green, was to advance from W51 trench, take the complicated German trench system to its front and pass on through to take the German Fact and Fable trench, setting up a strong point to secure the right flank by developing the maze of German trenches.

When the German front and second line trenches had been secured, the 1st Queen's Westminster, commanded by Lt. Col. Shoolbred, was to advance from Y48 trench, pass between the

CHAPTER FIVE

London Fusiliers and the Queen Victorias and make for the Quadrilateral, where they would link up with the 1st Sherwood Foresters.

The 1st Kensingtons, commanded by Lt. Col. Young, were to advance in support of the London Scottish. 'A' Company and parts of 'C' and 'D' Company were to construct a communication trench, with the aid of the Cheshire Pioneers and Engineers, between the two front lines in no man's land, constructing firing steps to the right. This working party was to be covered by snipers and their observers secured by the Sappers' wiring party.

At this stage in the war Battalion numbers were varied. Men were added and taken away almost on a daily basis – after any battle numbers dropped alarmingly, to the extent that at some stages Battalions were combined to make a fighting unit. As a rough estimate it would be safe to consider a Battalion as comprising four companies, each made up of two hundred men and within this, divided into squads of about fifty.

Part of The Kensington 'B' Company and two sections of Headquarter bombers were to clean up the trenches left by the London Scottish of any lingering Germans. The remainder of 'B' Company was to act as a carrying party to move forward ammunition and bombs. Meanwhile most of 'C' and 'D' Companies were kept in reserve lending a hand to keep the London Scottish supplied. Both the London Scottish and the Kensingtons were to protect the right flank from German penetration.

On the face of it this is a very sensible plan and considering the artillery supplied, quite feasible. But like all plans it didn't allow for what the opposition was likely to do, or for unknown circumstances. The Germans were never going to sit idly by and allow their deep galleried trenches protected by machine guns to be overrun. After all, their artillery was larger, better designed and more modern, with better-trained gun crews.

As observed by General Snow, there was a gap between the 56th and the 10th Division attacking Serre. These were the neighbouring troops a mile away on their right. If the British could take the German trenches quickly, after the artillery had done its job, all would be well.

CHAPTER SIX

THE NORTH MIDLANDERS

General Rawlinson believed that the only way he would be able to make sure his orders were being carried out was by incessant hard training to make sure the participants did everything strictly by rote. He planned for his Big Push to 'operate like clockwork, relying on detailed planning and continual practice; two operations that were going to win him the battle. Especially now, when he was dealing with Territorial soldiers... who might not be up to it'.

The British effort was going to be preceded by a five-day bombardment designed to achieve maximum destruction. An hour before the advance, smoke shells were to be fired and the German front line would receive its final onslaught from the massed guns. From then on, the artillery were going to lay down a creeping barrage 100 yards ahead of the first leading wave to keep the Germans' heads down. Further waves of riflemen were going to give support, clear the taken trenches and bring up supplies.

The infantry would advance in regularly spaced waves, 100 yards apart, five yards between each man, each Company to follow one after another with their Captain and Lieutenants

CHAPTER SIX

following their men. They were to occupy the German trenches, clear them and keep moving forward. All this movement was to be done according to the strict timetable, so that the leading waves of troops could take full advantage of the softening-up barrage. Support waves would consolidate and prepare for their next advance. This was not going to be like the child's game of 'What's the time Mr Wolf?' for there could be no stopping; they would have to keep up with the sequenced shelling. If the leading wave got too far forward their own guns would be firing on them. If too far back, the Germans would be up out of the dugouts firing at them.

Major General Wortley's 46th North Midland Division included the 137th North and South Staffords and the 139th Sherwood Foresters. They would lead the attack on the north side, supported by the 138th Lincolnshires and Leicestershires.

That May the 139th Sherwood Foresters held the Divisional front line at the village of Foncquevillers, burying new telephone cable lines, stacking ammunition, constructing gun pits and setting up observation posts, all in preparation for the coming battle. Directly to their front the enemy lines were held by the 3rd Battalion of the 91st Reserve Regiment, part of the 2nd Guard Reserve Division, all part of Stein's XIV Reserve Corps. The 9th and 12th Companies of the 3rd Battalion were the Sherwoods' immediate enemy, commanded by Leutnant der Reserve Metzner and Leutnant der Reserve Overesch.

The 46th Division's front line ran half a mile north of Hébuterne, then 800 yards beyond the left flank of the Sherwood Foresters. The village of Foncquevillers was directly opposite Gommecourt Wood. Here no man's land was about

CHAPTER SIX

400 yards wide, holding the ruins of the Sucrerie, a disused sugar beet factory then in ruins, twenty yards from the D6 main road.

Northwards, towards Monchy-au-bois, was in German hands. The village of Foncquevillers held the centre of the 46th Division's position directly opposite Gommecourt, its Park and Wood. Further north was the German gun position in Pigeon Wood, not far from the salient of trenches called the 'Little Z' stationed on the British Divisions' left flank. This part of the German line was called the Schwalben Nest, and it held a Maxim gun able to enfilade the whole of the German line to the east. The previous winter, the occupying British troops had come to the conclusion that they were too weak to hold all the line, so they selected certain parts for fortifying, wiring them into strong points, then filling in the remainder with loose wire. In time this became weighed down by the weight of the collapsing sides of the trench.

The village of Foncquevillers was in a better state of preservation than Hébuterne. It was at least recognisable as a former place of habitation, having most of its buildings still standing. The brick-built church was still there, even if the clock had stopped at 11.45. Its crypt housed the Battalion ammunition store and the mill's cellar the Company Office. The village boasted a YMCA where food could be bought to supplement the boring army rations. It could even be described as a good billet.

The brick cottages with their boundary walls gave shelter to their kitchen gardens containing vines and apple orchards. Beyond the patch of grass outside the orchard the ground

CHAPTER SIX

dipped down to no man's land, where work was in progress every night digging a new forward trench, a move guaranteed to give a 100-yard start to the attacking Midlanders all along the sector. This was in keeping with the work being carried out by the 56th Division on their front.

The 137th and 139th Brigades moved forward into trenches opposite Gommecourt Park on the 4th June. In unison the 138th, the Lincolnshires and Leicestershires, moved back, keeping a supporting role. The thick woodland to their front had been interwoven by dense belts of barbed wire and further belts added in front of every German trench. The British field guns and mortars had great difficulty in cutting gaps. The German guns took the opportunity while the British guns were silent to register their guns on the communication trenches, stopping before the British guns could 'range-on'.

The British artillery batteries behind Foncquevillers began registering their guns on the 24th June, having been allocated 400 rounds per gun per day to cut through the wire and take out the German gun pits. This allocation was then increased to 700 rounds per day. Work on the gun pits had been suspended by the incessant rain, delaying the sighting of many of the guns. As no delay could be contemplated, the guns were set up in uncompleted pits. It was opportune that the German artillery was not too active as this was going on. The activity in the British rear was frantic as new rail trackways, metalled roads, store houses, ammunition and bomb dumps were created close to the front. Compounds were built for prisoners and the wounded.

General Snow's plan had the Sherwood Foresters' 1/7th

CHAPTER SIX

Battalion attacking as the first wave, with the 1/5th on their right. The 1/6th Battalion would bring up the rear in support of the two-Battalion attack and the 1/8th held in reserve to bring forward stores and ammunition. Five minutes before the attack opened, the smoke parties would discharge their smoke bombs and candles.

The 139th Brigade would attack with five waves made up of 'A', 'B' and 'C' Companies, having the Little Z on their left. The fourth would bring up the rear and convert the German front line trench by reversing the firing steps, and the fifth would hump stores and ammunition. 'A' Company were to kick off the battle from the newly-dug trench in no man's land, the other two, 'B' and 'C' would form up in the old trench and 'D' the 4th, occupying the retrenchment line, with the 5th in Green Street. There would have been about 200 men in each wave.

Gommecourt Park, most of the village and the Château were not to be attacked by the Foresters, for they were not to stop but to keep going, to meet up with the 56th coming from the other side of the Park. (An order of the day requested attacking Battalions to keep back one Company from each Battalion from all future attacks, to act as a reserve and core for a future retraining programme in times when the bulk of the Battalion had been lost.)

The Brigade's targets were the German trenches to their front, given the identifying names Food and Fork, between the Little Z on their right and the communication trench Orinoco, making for Pigeon Wood. To the left would be Little Z and the Schwalben Nest, a salient sticking out from the line, on the side of the main road leading from the North Foreland. This

CHAPTER SIX

salient step in the line would present a danger if it were not eliminated by the main bombardment, for it would allow the Germans to enfilade the attacking force by providing a clear line of fire on the Sherwoods' left flank. As it turned out no special attention was given to this by the planners, which was to be a terrible mistake.

'A' Company lost practically all their men immediately, as soon as they emerged from their trench. A number of 'B' and 'C' made it to the German front line A, allowing twelve men to carry on to the German second line B. A number of attempts were made to rally the men, but exhaustion caused by the previous day's march back to the lines, atrocious weather conditions, flooded trenches and unbroken wire defeated them. Their spirits were not to be revived.

'The Kensingtons were the first of the 4th London Brigade to report their mobilization complete' declares Sergeant Bailey in the book *The Kensingtons*. Battalion Orders were received to prepare for Foreign Service on 28th October, 1914. On Sunday 3rd November the Battalion followed the band to Watford Station to board train for Southampton to take up station on their steam ship SS *Matheran*, bound for Le Havre and Rest Camp No. 1.

Even before mobilization they were a well-trained formation. The previous four months' experience marching from Watford, sailing to France, manning a front-line trench and undergoing all the rigours of trench life had made them incomparable veterans. Its four Companies had seen a lot of action, thankfully losing few men but maintaining a high proportion of their original pre-war volunteers.

CHAPTER SIX

On the 18th November, one half of the Battalion found itself occupying a trench south-east of Fauquissart. From the 21st their duties were shared with the other half in a three-day rota system. The Kensingtons' first battle was Neuve Chapelle, where they acted as Brigade Reserve. From the middle of March 1915 the Battalion was to share all the hazards of regular formations, for their baptism of fire was now over.

Each of the Battalions prided itself on representing a particular part of London. Sir Arthur Conan Doyle has Sherlock Holmes characterize a stockbroker's clerk who appears in one of his cases as 'representative of the type found in one of our better London Volunteer regiments'. Each Battalion prided itself on a core which represented a particular part of London. Within the London Division were Brigades, each comprising a number of Battalions overseas, headquarters or in training. Each Battalion had four rifle Companies made up of three platoons, comprising a number of squads. These multiples could be increased to four or more in times of war and shed in times of peace. After each battle the fighting strength of a platoon was made good by stripping away from the Headquarters Company.

To specify exactly the strength of each during an engagement is impossible. Accurate figures can be found only via the diary of each company, and these are not always available. Each Battalion had a number of other companies in support of the riflemen, who were in the front line. These were headquarters staff, transport, armourer, catering and other specialists, ie machine gun, mortar or bomb. Backing up the front-line troops were the reserves, support companies, ammunition parties, signallers, stretcher-bearers (band members) and pioneers.

When the Kensington Battalion took over the trenches at

CHAPTER SIX

Hébuterne from the 8th Middlesex on the 21st May, communication trenches had been established. The ruins of the village provided some cover from German snipers in Gommecourt Park, although it was within range of the German artillery in their rear. Battalion Headquarters was established in the mill's cellars, whose entrance was well sandbagged to protect against enemy fire.

It was obvious to all the men that an attack was imminent. The stacks of supply dumps, additional ammunition and bombs, new pipelines and railway tracks, road works and gun-pits were everywhere. The weather was glorious, allowing the preparation to be made in near-perfect conditions. However, this was not to last.

A draft of 200 men went some way towards making up for men lost. Behind the village, dumps were being laid out for ammunition and shells and guiding tapes laid for other supplies. By this time the Battalion, in company with the rest of the Brigade, knew that a trench was to be dug in no man's land. The digging parties were all supplied with the necessary picks, shovels and sandbags. At night parties went out to cut lanes in the British wire in preparation and lay tapes.

The British front line, prior to the construction of the new trench, was initialled as Sector Y: 50, 49, 48, 47, & W: 50, 49, 48. It then crossed the D27 main road. Lt-General Snow gave the task of constructing a new British front line trench to Brigadier General Loch. It was to be dug halfway between the British and German lines and identified with the letter S instead of R. This new front line was provided with communication trenches that linked the rear areas to the village of Hébuterne and Brigade Headquarters in the mill.

CHAPTER SIX

The 56th Division (three Brigades totalling 3000 men) was ordered to construct this new forward line in no man's land, 400 yards in front of the existing trench. This was to extend for almost two miles, the work being done on the nights of the 25th 26th May and identified with the omission of the old front lines' identification letter S.

The Germans observed all this activity but did nothing about it, not appreciating its significance. They kept well down behind their trench wall to shelter from a huge barrage, partly meant to achieve a distraction from what was going on. This new advanced trench was dug with little loss of life, which was a fine achievement. Volunteers were called for within the 167th to man the trench that night.

The following night the trench was deepened and firing steps cut in. This action saved many lives. This very simple expediency, like linking shell holes or pushing out a sap (trench), allowed attacking troops to get closer to the enemy front line. It was a pity that the new trench on the 46th front was so inadequate.

This trench building was no mere casual arrangement but a well-organized undertaking. The task was given artillery support if necessary and there were a number of ruses to confuse the Germans while the work was under way, like trailing empty cans behind a cart to mask the noise of digging. Its construction went a long way towards the successful penetration of the German front line on the day of the battle. On the days before and during the attack the 167th Brigade stood guard in this trench, staying until relieved by the 168th and 169th Brigades before the attack on the 1st July.

The 46th Division made an effort to do the same, but their

CHAPTER SIX

trench did not have the same support. Their poor attempt was undermined by the two days of incessant rain which half-filled the trench. These new advanced trenches were dug with little loss of life, which was a fine achievement. The following night the trenches were deepened and firing steps cut in.

The German front-line trench was sectioned off and given a code name beginning with the letter 'F' and the connecting trenches names beginning with 'E'. Behind this forward trench was the German second line, also identified with a letter 'F' for Fable and a new third rear trench close to the D6 main road.

The British artillery behind Hébuterne and Foncquevillers started registering their pieces on the 24th June, the object being to sever and flatten the wire while taking out the plotted German strong points.

As the day of the battle approached the bombardment intensified. The Germans noted where the guns were firing from, but did nothing. Prior to the battle all the communication trenches were made 'up' trenches until after the initial waves had gone forward. It was made clear that the previous direction for each communication trench would then be returned to its original task. This order was to lead to a terrible confusion when the wounded were being ferried back and Company runners tried to get through with their orders.

CHAPTER SEVEN

THE ATTACK

This is a Roll Call of active Kensington Officers who took part in the battle on 1st July 1916. In all there were 23,615 men of all ranks involved in the attack. The commanding officer was Lt-Colonel W H Young, who had been attached to the Battalion only two days before. He was stationed at Battalion HQ, organizing support. Second in command was Major Mackenzie. Senior Major Cedric C Dickens' adjutant was Lt C N C Howard, Transport Officer was Lt. Holland, Medical Officer was Lt. Keen, Quartermaster was Lt. Ridley, plus Drum-Major Skinner. All bandsmen were the Battalion's stretcher bearers.

OC 'A' Company: Captain Robertson, Lieutenants Lewin and Venables, 2nd Lts. Mager & Sach.

OC 'B' Company: Captain H. N. Whitty, Lieutenants Roseveare and Penn, 2nd Lt. Pike.

OC 'C' Company: Captain Ware (k), Lieutenants Cohen and Heath, 2nd Lt. Mason.

OC 'D' Company: Captain Taggart (w), Lieutenant Parton, 2nd Lt. Beggs.

The Pioneer Battalions were created in 1914 as a new concept in the British Army, with a role to provide the Royal

CHAPTER SEVEN

Engineers with skilled labour and to relieve the infantry from some of its non-combatant duties. Pioneers became the workhorses of the Expeditionary Force and acted in conjunction with the army constructing roads and bridges, working on entrenchments and fortifications, making mines and constructing approaches. They were provided with proper clothing, hatchets, saws, axes, spades and entrenching tools.

The Coldstream Guards and over three dozen County regiments created at least one pioneer Battalion. Several new Army Battalions were raised specifically as Pioneers, while others were converted Territorials or Kitchener units formed originally as conventional infantry.

The Pioneers adopted a badge of a cross rifle and pick. They wired no man's land, dug trenches and revetted in all weathers and in all terrains. On many occasions later in the war, they abandoned their working tools and fought alongside the infantry, repelling enemy attacks.

The work of the Pioneer Battalions has been largely ignored or misunderstood. In their efforts to stem the German offensives of 1918, several Pioneer units fought themselves to virtual annihilation. Far from being the units of the old and infirm, these 68 Battalions played a major role in the Allied victory.

A detail of the 5th Cheshire Pioneer Battalion, attached to the 56th Division, was to construct strong points in the German trenches, turning the firing positions to face the opposite direction towards the Germans' new front line. On the right flank the Kensingtons 'A' Company and Pioneers were to dig a new flank-facing trench under Major Dickens' leadership. A platoon of pioneers was detailed off to wire up the German side of the trench when completed, the whole covered by snipers with their observers.

CHAPTER SEVEN

The Royal Engineer detachment was responsible for making sure the British wire barrier to the front had been opened sufficiently for the troops to advance and the German wire gapped to allow the infantry to carry through to take the German frontline trench. There was a problem in that the gaps were too narrow. Bangalore torpedoes were used the night before to ensure breaches were made. As soon as the charge went up the Germans not only knew what was afoot but were given a chance to fix their machine-gun lines on the gaps before the troops could reach them. Just like the artillery bombardment and the creeping barrage, it was all a matter of timing. If you got it wrong, men were going to die.

In 1916 military communications were provided by the Royal Engineers Signal Service (the Royal Corps of Signals was formed in 1920). Communications in the front line area were maintained by using line and telephone between forward positions and formation headquarters.

To mask what was going on a screen of smoke was laid down by smoke shells and mortar bombs. This did not stop the Germans knowing an attack was likely to be made, but it did instil confidence in the advancing troops and save lives. However, as on the 56th front, the smoke was so thick that they could not see the gaps in the wire or know which way to turn. It took a few moments for the Company Sergeants to direct the men to the gaps.

Effective officer control is necessary for orders to be received and understood. In the case of the 56th this happened as planned and all was well. In the case of the 46th, however, more smoke was not made, and the men were mown down.

CHAPTER SEVEN

During the battle, information about what was happening to the advancing troops was relayed by a runner attached to the senior field officer. This would probably be the Company runner. The Captain would be stationed behind his Company as it was moving forward. Once the runner had left with a message, subsequent messages had to be sent by a rifleman who might not know where the Company or Headquarters was stationed.

It would take at least half an hour to get an answer. Signalling by flag was out of the question. Once the field telephone lines were snagged, torn or cut, resighting the artillery to take on specific targets became impossible to order. Someone who could give instructions to the gun layer had to see the fall of shot to be sure of a straddle – one shot over and one shot short.

Once the men had begun to advance, Headquarters would have very little idea how the battle was progressing. Spotting from the air was the only recourse, but in this instance the smoke was so thick nothing could be seen. Unless the advancing troops could take out the machine gun nests themselves the battle would be lost. In many instances these nests were eliminated through acts of heroism.

This was going to be biggest battle so far conceived to take the strain off the French, who were beginning to buckle at Verdun. The artillery had bombarded the German trenches with continuous fire for weeks. Most men thought it inconceivable that the artillery could not achieve what it had set out to do. They had faith in their officers, who had told them it was going to be a walkover. After all, the planning of every detail must have been covered - surely?

CHAPTER SEVEN

As daylight began to break on the horizon the men in the front-line trenches prepared themselves. Some washed, some shaved and others repacked their packs and collected all their things around them. Breakfast was consumed and hot tea drunk. They checked their possessions for the umpteenth time. The men nervously chatted about anything and everything with much false laughter and bonhomie.

Now the guns spoke again. It was rapid fire, a last period of hate which obliterated the German lines in lightning flashes, plumes of smoke and fountains of flung soil. The earth began to trickle once more from the sides of the trench as the ground quivered. It was hell on earth. They wondered if the wire in front of them had been broken and the machine-gun nests destroyed. They would soon find out.

At 0726 the British gunners discharged the last rounds of their preparatory barrage. Now they concentrated on producing a smoke-screen, a combination of explosive shells and smoke bombs calculated to cause maximum effect. Special sections on both the 46th and 56th fronts were lighting smoke candles and firing smoke bombs from mortars. A dense cloud of smoke drifted about in no man's land. The final loosing of shells heralded the start of the attack.

The men in the firing line had never experienced anything like such ferocity, for they felt it through their feet. Those on the firing steps could see the trees in the wood hurled about like twigs in an autumn gale. In the final minutes the trench mortars contributed a further last few rounds of smoke bombs as Gommecourt disappeared in a white mist of flaming shot and shattered vegetation. It appeared a total saturation, which could not be withstood.

CHAPTER SEVEN

The men waiting to go over the top were lulled into a false sense of security. Their officers had told them that it was going to be, literally, a walkover. They were equipped for such an event, being loaded down with all that would be needed to pursue the enemy. Duckboards were carried to bridge the trenches, they had food, water, ammunition, bombs, spare drums and belts for the machine guns, everything for a stay of three days before relief got to them.

The average load was sixty pounds plus the rifle. The supporting troops also had picks and spades to alter the German trench and do the necessary repairs, while stretcher bearers and engineers brought up the rear to give succour, support and communication. They had practised often and now it was the time to put their practice into action. No two men had exactly the same kit to go over the top with. Some had ladders, some bombs, others spare ammunition and water.

Company runners may have carried baskets of pigeons and signallers their flags. The Royal Engineers attached to the forward troops carried spare cable and tools for repairing breaks in the telephone wire. It was not envisaged by the commanders that the attacking force was likely to return the same day. The plan was to hold the taken German positions for a number of days until the supporting troops from the rear had regularised their positions.

The relevant Headquarter victualling sergeants had prepared a special breakfast and passed out bread and bully beef to sustain the men until the cookhouse staff could join the forward troops and set up their stoves.

On the north side the 5th Leicester held the British front line

CHAPTER SEVEN

south of Foncquevillers. They had moved into their trenches on 4th June, patrolling at night to check that the Germans were not preparing to attack or put out their own patrols.

The Germans had been faced with days of similar bombardments, forewarning them of an attack, so they were on their toes as soon as the artillery stopped. The machine-gun crews practised setting up their pieces in three minutes flat and were told that they were the saviours of their position. Lookouts were posted, using their periscopes to give the alarm in time. When the British smoke-screen was laid the alarm was given. Now was the time to put their practice into good use.

The Sherwood Foresters had never felt such an effect before. The ground was trembling and the trench sides were trickling with streams of dislodged earth. The puddles in the trench bottoms lapped about over the duckboards. Those brave or stupid enough to glance over the parapet could see the wood to their front disintegrating – trees being hurled into the air and branches being snapped off and flung about.

At 0730 the smoke bombs and explosive shells stopped. Section leaders shouted as the Staffords began to scramble out on to the parapet to form up, port arms and start to walk towards the enemy down the sloping ground into no man's land. As the Company Sergeants lent a hand to get the men out of the trench to form the second wave, the first had cleared the last of the British wire. The next wave was struggling out of the trench, some up ladders, others climbing on boxes, while the sergeants grabbed their equipment, helping all to form up.

So far all was going well. The men kept station as they

CHAPTER SEVEN

made their way through the smoke into Gommecourt Wood. Now they could feel the wind getting up, blowing the smoke away and thinning it sufficiently for the Germans to see the long lines of troops coming towards them. This prompted several Germans to clamber out of their trenches without their equipment and rush forward with their hands in the air.

On the other side of the park the London Rifle Brigade were doing the same thing. Long lines of men were making sure they were in position, walking quickly and quietly through the gaps in their own barbed wire, made the night before using Bangalore torpedoes. Just after 0700 on 1st July German observation posts on their right front, manned by the German 91st Reserve Regiment, reported that a smoke-screen was being laid down.

As the rest of the British Divisions advanced, the Kensingtons on the far side of the 56th Division held back, waiting for the London Scottish to move forward a hundred yards before they too formed up to follow on. Though the German wire had been gapped and the smoke-screen laid down, the German machine guns had reaped a terrible harvest. Even so, the dogged London Scottish had by 0800 penetrated the German line. They were the first of the 56th Division to move into and past the first German trench. In spite of the terrible fire, the men went forward, trying to keep in line at a steady pace.

The German wire was supposed to have been cut by the artillery fire, but in many places it was untouched. The strands caught in their equipment or became wrapped around their legs. It was discovered later that the Germans had moved back to their rear trenches.

CHAPTER SEVEN

Onward marched the London Scottish to take and move past the German second line, making for the other side of the maze of enemy trenches and Fable and the German third trench. The advance continued until all the German trenches on the right flank of Gommecourt were in British hands.

Part of the 169th Brigade, the Queen's Westminster Rifles, followed up, moving up over the captured German trenches between the London Rifles and Queen Victoria's to start the linking-up movement with the North Midland Division when they moved down from the north. As this was happening, a section of the Cheshire Pioneers was constructing strong points in the German trenches and repositioning the firing steps to face the Germans' new front line. The Westminsters had received many casualties from bypassed Germans who were emerging from their deep dugouts and shooting them in the back. As the German artillery began to realise what was happening they started shelling no man's land and their own abandoned front line.

As there were no officers available to direct the bombing to clear the German dugouts, second lieutenant George Arther left his Pioneer Section to take over the attack. Though slightly wounded he instilled resolution in the men about him. Forcing their way forward, the bombers got to within 400 yards of the German trench, almost within reach of the point where they were to join up with the North Midland Division. Meanwhile the British Artillery bombardment was directed on to the German artillery to act as a counter battery. They in turn were replying, shooting into no man's land and disrupting the supply of ammunition and bombs, which made the British advance difficult through lack of support, there being a shortage of ammunition and bombs.

CHAPTER SEVEN

Fortunately for the Germans, the right sector of their fire trenches facing the 46th North Midland Division was not being shelled. This allowed the sheltering Germans there to leave their deep dugouts to see what was going on. The ground to their front looked towards no man's land and Foncquevillers, a distance of just over 400 yards. The surface was level, gradually dipping down into no man's land and giving them a completely open vista. They could see the smoke-screen being blown about, thinning in some places and clearing in others. Through these gaps the British North Midlanders could be seen coming towards them.

The Germans set off their alarms and their trenches began to fill with breathless men. Those manning the Maxim machine guns had to assemble them and arrange their ammunition to be close at hand. The order was given for rapid fire.

The London men were ordered to attack and the section leaders shouted to the men to form up. Long lines of men set off, making sure they were in line, keeping five yards between each as they walked through the gaps in their own barbed wire made the night before.

The British artillery bombardment had been lifted to raise their sights to the next aiming point. The London Division's advance was downhill into a shallow valley, then up the other side towards the village towards the road, Nameless Farm and finally the Quadrilateral. The attack was across open ground enfiladed by German machine guns and artillery. All troops were told to advance at walking pace, keep in a straight line and not to bunch up.

CHAPTER EIGHT

THE GERMAN RESPONSE

Manning the German Line before the 56th Division was the 91st Reserve Regiment. Their lookout men had not been so observant, and this, coupled with a thick smoke-screen, completely masked what the British troops were doing. This slow reaction meant the Germans took longer to man their trenches and erect their machine guns, allowing the 56th Division to make particularly good progress.

The previous night a number of British patrols had blown gaps in the German wire with Bangalore torpedoes, which helped enormously the next day. By 0800 the bulk of the 56th were in the German front line trenches taking prisoners, while others had even gone further into the German support trenches beyond.

On the left flank of the 46th Divisions Front the 5th and 7th Sherwood Foresters had risen up out of their front line trenches and formed up. They felt confident that their gunners had done a fine job. Their officers had been telling them for weeks that the bombardment had flattened the German trenches and there would be no opposition. They did as they were instructed and marched forward, finding gaps in the wire, and entered the

CHAPTER EIGHT

Gommecourt wood, after having first moved past the maze of forward German front line trenches. They were making for the Quadrilateral, the heart of the Kern Redoubt.

Following orders, they were not stopping but leaving the passed-over trenches to be mopped up by the later waves following on. They were not to know that the wind had risen and driven the smoke-screen away, revealing the follow-up waves to the Germans. These men of the Sherwood Foresters were never seen again.

As another wave of the Sherwoods left their trenches the German field guns, stationed at Monchy further to the north, were now alerted to the fact that an attack was on. They joined in the machine gun fire enfilading from the Schwalben Nest (Little Z) and those from the German front line. The enemy field guns, previously laid down onto the communication trenches and no man's land, plastered these positions. The British carrying parties, heavily loaded down, were caught in the middle, not knowing whether to go forward or back. The machine-gun fire decimated them as they tried to move.

On the 46th right flank, on either side of the D6 main road, the first two waves of the South and North Staffordshires were held up, finding no gap in the German wire, particularly around the Sucrerie. The slaughter was enormous as the men were trying to clamber over the dead, dying and wounded, many impaled on the wire. Universally it was the officers and rallying Sergeants who were killed, leaving the men without orders or leadership. Those who did finally find a gap and sought cover in the wood were rounded up by the now fully alerted German defenders.

CHAPTER EIGHT

'A' Company of the Leicestershires, plus two other platoons and their leading Sub-Lieutenants, started out to make their way to the Sucrerie to begin to construct a communication trench stretching to the German front line. They started to mark out the extent it was to take. It was a hopeless task, as the German machine guns were continually raking the ground around and forcing them to take cover. It became painfully obvious that it was a hopeless task and the detailed troops were ordered back to the start line. There they found the Staffordshires waiting for the order to make another attempt to move forward into the wood.

To the south, on the other side of Gommecourt, the 56th support Companies were advancing to join those which had been first in the German Line. The German artillery now took up the challenge. A move was made to stabilize the capture of the German second line by the Pioneers. All the German trenches were now in British hands.

The Queen's Westminster Rifles continued moving through the London Rifles to start the linking-up movement with the North Midland Division moving down from the north. The London Scottish on the extreme right also made excellent progress towards the main road, where they were to set up a strong point.

After having their rum issue the Queen Victorias stood to until 0725, when they put up a smoke-screen. At 0730 they went over the top, with the London Scottish and Queen's Westminster Rifles bringing up the rear. They took four lines of trenches from the Germans, but were driven back by midday to their original position. Losses were very heavy, though they took many prisoners.

CHAPTER EIGHT

The Germans made a special effort to kill all those men directing, marshalling and leading the attack. These officers and leading NCOs were easily identifiable, for they wore smarter uniforms and carried walking sticks and side arms. The Germans were so adept at doing this that attacking forces soon lost all their commanding officers and NCOs. In proportion far more replacement officers were needed. In many cases men of lesser rank took on superior jobs.

By late morning, part of the Kensington Battalion on the right flank of the line was about to dig a connecting trench in no man's land. The London Rangers and Queen Victorias were on their left, making for the third rear German trench, Nameless Farm and the main road.

The X Corps of Lt General Hunter-Weston at Serre, a mile away on the 56th Division's right flank, had been pushed back. When the attack petered out the German artillery switched their sights on to no man's land and W Sector trench behind the London Scottish. It was here that the rest of the Kensingtons were preparing to make for no man's land led by Major Dickens, after being told the London Scottish had passed the first two German trenches to start digging the connecting trench.

The Germans shelled this trench to such a degree that the Kensingtons lost half their men. Very few had even the opportunity to get out of the trench. The Kensingtons' sector trench W48R was only four feet wide and packed with soldiers who were unable to move because it was so full of dead, dying and wounded men.

Major Dickens sent back word at 1310 hours that there were few men left to hold their existing position and that he

CHAPTER EIGHT

was the only officer left. Could he please have instructions? The Kensingtons lost sixteen officers and 300 men. Among those killed was the battalion second-in-command, Major Mackenzie, who was leading the Kensingtons on the battlefield. From about midday this responsibility passed to Major Dickens (a year previously Dickens had been Captain of A Company). Major Dickens was killed by a sniper eight weeks later.

To the north things were going from bad to worse. The 46th Division had started off, but had been defeated by the German barbed wire, which had not been gapped. The previous night's rain had turned their trench into a morass and some of the men were knee-deep in mud all night long. It was difficult to get the second wave of men out in time. As they appeared in dribs and drabs on the top, they were machine-gunned down on top of others who were trying to get out. The slipping, clawing men could not get a hold of the trench side, for the dead and wounded were blocking the ladders. There were long rows of dead and dying men piling up on the parapet, making it even more difficult.

The officers were standing on the parapet, helping men out and ordering others to support the men in front. Another wave of men was ordered forward, only to be mown down again. By this time men were refusing to move, staying with the wounded and huddled together in shell holes.

Further north in the centre, things were a little better. The Germans there had not been so quick, allowing the Sherwood Foresters to get into the front line trench, clear it and make towards the support line. The Germans erected a machine gun

CHAPTER EIGHT

facing to their rear, back on to their own lines, which took the attackers in the rear. By the end of the morning their trenches were clear. A sortie was made by the Lincs and Leics. Late in the day they were to seek stragglers and survivors, but in the end they had to give up and return to their own lines.

The previous day it had been suspected by the Germans that the British were going to attack, but they did not know exactly when. The British preparations had always been made obvious, suggesting a main attack to divert attention away from Rawlinson's 'Big Push'. This ruse was having the desired effect.

The 91st German Reserve Regiment, on the north side of Gommecourt Park, had the luck to find the smoke-screen patchy at best and non-existent in places. They were rightly alarmed, and used their practice and preparations to man their front line and prepare for hostilities.

The Germans easily repelled the invaders, gunning down the waves of troops coming towards them. The North Midlanders were not a serious threat, even though many limited assaults were made throughout the day. Those who had made it faced almost immediate expulsion.

Conditions in the trenches on the 46th Division's front were horrific. The German field guns had bracketed the area and the trench was full of the dead and dying. Those who were still active were crouching down, too exhausted to make any move. At 1530 the British artillery resumed their bombardment to prepare the way for a renewed attack. Major General Wortley came forward to see that his order was carried out.

The Sherwood Foresters started out again, adopting the same tactics. On their right they expected to see the

CHAPTER EIGHT

Staffordshires, but the latter had refused to move and were not accompanying them, so they were on their own. The order was given once again to return to the old front line. The attack had been a failure. By 1600 all that was left of the Staffordshires were ordered back out of line and the 5th Leicestershires took over. On their left the 5th Lincolnshires did a similar job, relieving the Sherwood Foresters.

On the London Division's front it was a different story. The smoke-screen had been more than sufficiently laid by the Royal Engineers and did all that it was supposed to do. The London Rifles, Queen Victoria's, Irish Rangers and London Scottish, had all penetrated into the German lines, helped by the bombardment and smoke-screen. The Westminsters worked their way through The Rifles and Victorias into the German third trench and The Kensingtons followed on, after the London Scottish. All found the smoke-screen almost impenetrable, having been laid so thickly that some of the forward British troop became lost and disorientated.

By 0830 the 56th Division was well on its way. They made for the D6 road trench, jumping into the German front line (F) and working their way forward through the communication trenches. Many of the dazed Germans were captured and led back. All along the trench mini battles were raging as the parties bombed each other.

At 0900 the first objectives had been reached and the leading British troops had penetrated over a mile towards the Kern redoubt, where they were to link up with the North Midlanders. On the Londoners' left was Gommecourt Park and village, on the right Nameless Farm on the D6 Hébuterne-Fuquay Road and

CHAPTER EIGHT

a little further, the maze of German trenches which were to be made into a strong point by the London Scottish.

Now the German 170 Reserve Regiment (52nd Division) prepared to counter-attack. Von Below arrange for 55 Reserve Regiment to attack with four companies to the north and nine companies to the south, including two from the 2nd Guards Reserve. By midday and early afternoon the impact of this counter-attack began to be felt. The first things to be destroyed by the Germans were the barricades erected by the Pioneers and Engineers, allowing them to retake their old trench.

The whole London Division was now beginning to run out of bombs and ammunition. The German artillery was ordered to shell no man's land. Little by little the British were put under pressure, giving up well earned territory. Pockets of desperate troops sheltered in shell-holes, which provided some respite from the machine guns and barrage. The German 2nd Guards Reserve Division, having been pushed back almost out of the salient, were now recovering, still holding Fricourt in the front line. What was left of the Kensingtons, including part of the London Scottish machine gun section, was preparing to repel any German foolish enough to try to take it back. Four hours on they were still in position, although by now the Westminsters had been pushed back to the first line along with the bulk of what was left of the Division.

The diversionary tactics formulated by the British Headquarters Staff were working, diverting German efforts on to their front in accordance with the original plan. Now the Germans, having destroyed the 31st Division at Serre on the Kensingtons' right, relayed their guns to shell no man's land

CHAPTER EIGHT

on the Kensingtons' front which was nearest to them.

As the 46th was enfiladed, so was the 56th. It was a devastating barrage. It fell like a 'curtain of steel', writes Christopher Moore in *Trench Fever*. No man's land was cut off. Major Dickens and his men could receive no help from reserves or stretcher bearers, for they were stuck out in front with very little cover having to suffer the awful bombardment.

Now the situation to the right of the 56th was becoming untenable. The prime object had been achieved. Linking up with the 46th would have been helpful in straightening up the line, but taking on a very strong trench and dugout system which was still in good working order, without reserves, could and would be described as rash. The worst option was to do nothing, for the Germans were beginning to take stock and recover fast.

On the 56th left, the Westminsters had moved up between the London Rifles and the Queen Victorias; they were prepared to start a bombing attack on the rear of the Gommecourt garrison. Unfortunately the Westminsters had received too many casualties and there was no one to direct the attack.

Leaving his pioneers, Second Lieutenant George Arther led the attack, though slightly wounded. Forcing their way forward, the bombers got to within 400 yards of the German third trench, almost within reach of where they were to join up with the North Midland Division.

The North Midlanders had fared badly and had been forced back. One or two groups were holding out against strong opposition. Once again they continued the attack to try and link up with the Westminsters, who were bombing their

CHAPTER EIGHT

way towards them.

General Snow demanded another attack, pressing the Divisional commander to order another attack using the supporting troops. Six Battalions of the 46th had started that morning and all had been driven back; there were only two companies left. Not a single officer had survived. Snow ordered the North Midlanders to repeat their attack that afternoon to link up with the London Division, which by then was being counter-attacked and was gradually being forced back to the captured German trench to their rear.

The Germans, on the other hand, were now over their initial shock and getting stronger by the minute. It did not take them long to understand the significance of the British plan. Not that they understood that the battle of Gommecourt was a diversionary attack; they thought these two divisions opposing were trying to encircle them. They had every intention of making sure that this did not happen. Now the German artillery behind Serre ranged in, joining those behind the Quadrilateral to bombard no man's land and the British front line.

Gradually the British troops began to run out of ammunition. Most of the senior officers who had set out in the morning were now either dead or injured. The afternoon wore on and the fighting continued. The pockets of resistance were getting smaller.

There were now 1700 men dead, 200 taken prisoner and over 2000 wounded. Most of these were lying about on the battlefield. The Germans systematically raked them with machine-gun fire to make sure there were no isolated pockets of resistance.

CHAPTER EIGHT

All around the wounded lay broken barbed wire, military equipment and the bodies of the dead and dying. Their task was to somehow crawl from hole to hole, skirting areas of water that were too deep and keeping below the sky-line. It was a miserable end to a bitter fight begun with such high hopes.

By late afternoon the guns of both sides had stopped firing. The odd casualty who was capable of movement began to crawl his way back. Stretcher-bearers from both sides were moving about among the wounded. The badly-injured were calling out, some for water, others for comfort. The parties of first-aiders gave succour to either side, making no distinction. There were 4749 casualties in the London Division alone, out of nearly 60,000 who had started out just over eight hours before.

As the afternoon wore on, fighting broke out again. Of the two Battalions on the right flank there were only four officers and seventy men remaining of the main attacking force to hold on to the German trenches. They had gathered together to hold a series of shell holes and half-built trenches. It was now touch and go as to whether there was going to be a total rout. One or two other smaller groups were making their way back, passing the dead and dying and giving hope to those remaining that they would be remembered.

The 46th Division, now back in their original front line positions, had come to the conclusion that their hope to link up with the 56th had to be abandoned. The first Company of the Sherwood Foresters had reached the German third line in the morning, capturing several prisoners, who in the end had to be released. Some of the men had reached the meeting-place surrounding the Quadrilateral.

CHAPTER EIGHT

Once the 31st Division had been driven away from Serre, the German guns could take up the battle against the 46th and swing round to the right, enfilading the remnants in no man's land. The 5th Lincolnshires, who had taken over the front, made another advance at midnight to give support to any Sherwood Foresters still holding out. They in turn were heavily resisted and lost many men.

Later still, when the light was poor, more stragglers started to drag themselves in. They were tired, hungry and distressed at having got so far and not in the end having succeeded. The Germans were again moving about in no man's land, not only finding their own wounded but directing their first-aiders and stretcher-bearers to find the English wounded too. This concern for the wounded was reciprocated. It was a seven to one battle in favour of the Germans. Both German and British stretcher parties would curse the state of the ground as they picked up the wounded and staggered off.

By the late evening a steady rain was falling. The cries and moans of the wounded could still be heard. Occasionally there would be the crack of a rifle shot. In the distance a flare would go up or there would be the louder bang of an artillery piece which shook the ground. It was no easy matter for the retiring sections to keep hidden.

On 2nd July much effort was made to tidy up the front line and collect the dead and wounded on both fronts. By 2100 on the second day the Leicesters were relieved by the London Rangers, who had moved over from the south.

What remained of the 46th Division marched back to Bienvillers au Bois, shepherding the late-comers still making

CHAPTER EIGHT

their way back from the battlefield. The Kensingtons were relieved that same night by the 8th Middlesex. Those who were left marched back to the old French trenches near Sailly au Bois, relieving the 4th Lincolns in trenches on the north side of Foncquevillers.

CHAPTER NINE

THE FINAL TALLY AND LESSONS LEARNED

The total casualties on the Somme were over 1.3 million, divided equally between the Allies and the Germans. The battle finally ended on the 14th November 1916, with British losses at 400,000. The 56th Division suffered grievously. The figures speak for themselves. The attack on The Kern Redoubt was successfully made the following year. The casualties on the first day of battle were:

1st London Rifles - 19 officers and 553 men
1st London Scottish - 14 officers 544 men
1st Queen's Westminsters - 28 officers and 475 men
1st Queen Victorias (estimated) - 20 officers and 400 men
1st Kensingtons - 16 officers and 300 men

Lt General Rawlinson attacked with thirteen divisions on a front fifteen miles long north of the River Somme, and the French with five divisions on an eight-mile front mainly south of the river, where the German defence system was less highly developed.

The unconcealed preparations on the Gommecourt front

CHAPTER NINE

and the long bombardment starting on the 24th June had given away any chance of surprise. This was part of the battle plan envisaged by Generals Haig and Rawlinson. Later findings confirm that the Germans knew they were going to be attacked and had a good idea when, how and why. Their knowledge and guesses confirm that the deception plan was working, which was in accordance with the wishes of the British General Headquarters and part of the grand strategy.

The more unsure and on edge the Germans were made to feel with numerous excursions to their front, the better. These diversions would help the main British attack, drawing away possible German attention, reserves and resources. No General worth his salt would plan a campaign without such a plan in place. This was not clever – it was just good military thinking.

The German troops taking part in the defence numbered 24,000 men. They suffered 601 casualties, including 185 killed. Most of the attacking British Battalions, each of about 800 men, lost half their strength.

According to Farrar-Hockley (see *The Somme*, 1966), on the morning of the 1st July at 0715 German observation stations reported a smoke-screen developing on both sides of the salient. Although the British bombardment had been intensified since 0625, the German fire trenches facing north-west, the Staffords' front, were not being shelled. Several German observers of the local 91st Reserve Regiment garrison came up from their deep dugouts to see what was happening. To their front, the ground ran level to the Staffords' lines 400-500 yards away beyond the village of Foncquevillers; on their right was the one-time Sucrerie.

CHAPTER NINE

Christopher Moore's *Trench Fever* states that by 0900 the commander of the Staffords, Brigadier-General Williams, knew that any of his men who survived would not resume the attack – they had had enough and many had been shot down like dogs.

The Fifth Leicesters who were there in support were told the artillery was being called for a further shoot and that his job was to organise another wave attack. Major-General Wortley personally took charge, realising that a firm hand was necessary to see that it was carried out.

The Sherwood Foresters were on the left and Staffords and Fifth Leicesters on the right. It was to be a repeat of the morning's attack, preceded by an artillery barrage and smoke-screen and planned for a 1215 start.

This new attack was delayed a number of times because the communication trenches were clogged up with the dead and wounded. Stretcher bearers were ferrying the injured away and resupply parties struggled forward, jostling each other as they tried to get past. All along the 46th front collapsed trenches were under shell fire. The previous heavy rain had washed away the battered sides, making the trench shallower.

At 1530 the British artillery commenced their bombardment and the few Stokes mortars added their smoke-screen. On the left the smoke was so thin that Brigadier Shipley of the Sherwoods ordered his men to stay where they were, knowing it would be slaughter if the attack went ahead. The Staffords, seeing that the Sherwoods were not getting out of their trenches and shell holes, refused to go forward, as did the Fifth Leicesters. It was stalemate - no-one moved.

The German artillery, being informed that the British

CHAPTER NINE

bombardment had started up again and a smoke-screen created, prepared to begin firing again. Now they were fully alert, thinking this was another attack. They redoubled their efforts, sending down a shrapnel barrage which caused even more casualties to the wounded men. Many huddled in shell holes waiting for a chance to get back to their lines, while the sheltering advancing troops waited for an inspired officer to lead them forward.

By 1600, Lt-General Snow knew that the 56th were being slowly pushed back and the 46th had stalled. He concluded that the attack to link up was not going to happen, so he instructed the attempt to be called off and the original British front line to be re-established and remanned. The diversion had been made and achieved, but the hope of joining up to straighten the line to eliminate the salient had to be abandoned. From now on there would be recriminations. Who was going to pay the price for failure was not so clear. Was it the plan, the planners or the poor bloody infantry?

Considering the attack had been purely a diversion and not meant as a break-out, the effort by the Territorials had been very costly. The Grand Plan to help the French was a noble one and its aim strategically necessary. However, war's simple object, to remove the enemy, had not been achieved.

Rawlinson's insistence on a lengthy bombardment to soften German resistance was an acceptable strategy, if it had been achieved. It was not, because the necessary weapons were not at hand. Haig had preferred a shorter preliminary bombardment and the adoption of skirmishing infantry tactics. This might have worked better, but it seems doubtful.

CHAPTER NINE

Haig's deferment to Rawlinson's greater experience and fears were in error. No front line soldier would ever limit artillery bombardment to his enemy given, the chance. However, this presupposes that the artillery would achieve all its targets and purposes. In this instance the artillery failed miserably. Their expertise at reducing specific targets was pathetic and their wire-cutting skills hopeless. They were not up to the task. This was not necessarily their fault - they were not properly trained, nor did they have the proper weapons or shells.

These deficiencies should have been exposed before the battle by Rawlinson. It was, after all, his plan. The artillery's goals were an integral part of this plan and achieving them was vital. The gunners were quite incapable of backing the infantry, although they thought at the time that they were doing a good job.

The observers could see the targets putting up a shower of earth, but this was simply surface material. The dug-in and reinforced bunkers and weapon pits were hardly being touched. The Germans, purposely alerted to the coming attack, had retired most of their troops back to the rear trenches, some even to the third trench, on the road. That the British had only 60 howitzers along the whole front speaks volumes, for only howitzers project shells to fall vertically, which is necessary to puncture dug-outs and penetrate the top cover to weapon pits.

According to Brigadier Scott's presentation 'Artillery Survey in World War 1' (2003) at Woolwich, Britain was not prepared for war in 1914. The artillery had 18-pounder guns and 4.5-inch howitzers with which to raise gun positions and men in dug-

CHAPTER NINE

outs. Such weapons are only suitable for targets in the open.

For the battle on the Somme, Rawlinson had only 105 heavy guns (Farrar-Hockley, *The Somme*, maintains it was 107) and howitzers by the previous June: 36 x 60-powder guns, 8 x 6-inch guns, 40 x old 6-inch howitzers, 4 x 8-inch howitzers, 14 x 9.2-inch howitzers and 3 x 15-inch howitzers. Scott maintains that the state of the maps was poor and that using flash-to-bang time measurement to determine range was inaccurate (Lt-General Allenby, commander of the British Third Army, later authorized a flash spotting course). The battle relied upon air reconnaissance to locate enemy guns. Commander Second Army decree that counter-battery work must be a matter chiefly for the heavy artillery and that enemy gun location should be allotted to the Artillery Intelligence Officer and his assistants attached to each Group Commander.

This bought into being the start of official counter-bombardment systems. By 1st July each army had a flash spotting Observation Section of the then 1 Field Survey Company continuously manned connected to observation posts by telephone. However, it took some time for the spotting information to be passed up to the Corps Counter-Battery Officer and down to a gun battery.

According to *Official History of the Great War* by Brigadier-General Sir James E Edmonds CB, CMG, Royal Engineers (retd), psc, the British guns fired 20,000 tons of metal from the start of the battle on the 24th, which constituted 1,627,824 shells of all types. Christopher Moore maintains in *Trench Fever* that perhaps a third were duds. What is clear from official records is that most of the shot was shrapnel unsuitable for raising dug-in positions.

CHAPTER NINE

Owing to the dense and rigid infantry tactics and the 'wave system' employed by Rawlinson, the losses were unnecessarily heavy. Rush and drop, cover and deploy, are the skills of a skirmisher using the terrain. Such tactics might have achieved more. In this instance, it would most certainly have been no worse and possibly better. Giving advancing troops the option of reaching a certain position using whatever tactics the situation demands on the day can have a better result, if resolutely carried out. It was in this that Rawlinson had his doubts. He believed the Territorials' resolve and skill was wanting. Rawlinson's wave system relied on the artillery laying down a creeping barrage before the leading troops to make the enemy drop down below their parapet. It was timed to the minute and applied to precede the first wave.

For this part of the plan to work efficiently the following troops must follow precisely. They should not be far enough forward to catch shot falling short, nor far enough behind to allow the Germans to pop up. The system could be made defunct in a number of ways: if the Germans gunned down the first wave the second might not move forward to cover the gap, if the wire was not cut, resulting in bunching up, if the terrain was shell holed, slippery, or covered by the dead and dying. Any or all of these would ensure the barrage would begin to be out of sync for the advancing first wave.

As a fundamental part of the battle plan and a way to get the troops to move forward, the wave system was useless and bound to break down. In battle fatigues with normal webbing pouches for spare ammunition, tirailleurs (mobile shooters) can move independently to meet with situations as they

CHAPTER NINE

appear. If, as in this case, the forward troops are weighed down by carrying too much equipment, freedom and flexibility of movement is placed in jeopardy. Supporting troops can bring forward any extra equipment needed, allowing the timetable for keeping up with the creeping barrage to be met.

Rawlinson also wrongly believed that the artillery would achieve its targets and keep the Germans' heads down. In this he was fundamentally wrong and guilty for not proving so himself. What he was planning – for the opposing guns to be eliminated and German troops to be cowed - was not possible using the weapons he had available, nor were the Germans daft enough to place themselves where they could be shelled, having been forewarned what was going to happen.

The smoke-screen was also a major infantry tactic, giving cover to those advancing and bringing dismay to those fearing discovery and surprise. Again this weapon was not universally efficient and effectual. Rawlinson turned down the idea of a night attack, fearing uncertainty at best and chaos at worst, once again fearing the poor training of the Territorials. His battle plan was based upon his army's lack of infantry expertise.

Rawlinson and his Headquarters had failed to recognise the depth and strength of the German trench system. They insisted on a wave system of attack, placing far too much reliance on his artillery and failing to understand its obvious limitations.

Planning diversions are a major part of any battle. Their usefulness can be outweighed if there are too many casualties or loss of equipment. Rawlinson did tell his commanders not to take their attack too far, nor to go forward without making sure the German trenches to their front were abandoned, for

CHAPTER NINE

there were no reserves or support for a follow-up. These flexible orders, relying upon individual decisions made in the heat of battle, are susceptible to hasty judgements. There is a tendency for commanders to become dogged and refused to give up even when retreat is the wisest option. It requires a strong leader to pull his troops back.

The fault was General Snow's in persisting in the attack. Rawlinson should have made sure his orders were obeyed. In the end, too much was asked of too few troops, relying on the unknown effects of prolonged shelling. The poor performance of the 46th Division can be attributed to bad preparatory work by the area commanders to make sure the barbed wire had been rendered useless to the defender.

There are no references to suggest efforts were made on the night before the battle to find out if there were gaps in the German wire, and if so where and how extensive they were. In the event that there were none, or not in the correct places, Bangalore torpedoes would be used before the troops made the attack the next morning. This essential check, to ensure the attack had a chance, seems elementary. Then lane markers were laid and their positions marked on maps for Battalion commanders. Sniper teams, to give the attackers cover, were an essential ingredient which also gave the advancing troops confidence.

The main aim of the attackers was to take the German front line, and for that to happen the troops of course had to reach it. The use of smoke, by shell, bomb and candle, to mask attacking waves was essential if there was a fear that the attackers were being watched by those who would prevent

CHAPTER NINE

them reaching the line, or if the smoke was so thick that the attackers could not see the man next to them.

Having smoke teams in no man's land to ensure suitable cover is a must if there is any prevailing wind, or if there is a possibility that the initial cover has been badly laid. The guiding tape-lines must be laid while it is still dark, before the last shell has dropped. There is no point laying cable and tape in no man's land if firing is still going on.

The new halfway trench dug on the 56th Hébuterne front should have been more carefully copied on the north. Raiding parties should have been sent out to create unease and uncertainty and more attention should have been paid to eliminating the machine gun nests at 'Z'. The North Midlands' strength and vigour prior to the attack had been severely strained by having to march backwards and forwards to practise at Lucheux and by the ghastly weather. Both added to their misery.

It was a seven-to-one battle in favour of the Germans. Both the 46th and 56th Divisions remained on the battlefield until October. The fact that the attack at Gommecourt did distract the Germans in the end made very little difference to the failed effort of the main battle. The first day's figures for casualties on the Somme were 57,470 men.

General Farrar-Hockley considered that they had not failed at all. Their task had not been to capture Gommecourt, perhaps the strongest position in the sector, but to divert upon themselves 'the fire of artillery and infantry which might otherwise be directed against the flank of the main attack near Serre'. However, pressure could still have been mounted to

CHAPTER NINE

ensure the ruse was believed, without the needless loss of the vast numbers of men. The point of all the attacks along the front was to take the strain away from the French. In this the battle on the Somme succeeded.

Martin Middlebrook maintains that with hindsight the battle should not have been waged at all, as both sides were locked in a stalemate and it would have taken a genius - and a brave man - to have spoken out. That is true but leaving hindsight aside, what occurred was unnecessary slaughter.

Rawlinson's wave theory was ridiculous, as was his reliance on the artillery to take out the German guns and machine gun pits and to break up the wire. The infantry were badly handled. Riflemen were sharpshooters, skirmishers or tirailleurs. On the day the Territorials acted like guardsmen without their irregular forward protectors.

Local area commanders should have made greater use of night patrols to inspect the state of the wire and the shell-holed landscape and see where cover and entry could best be found. Special units should have plotted where the static machine-gun nests were located, so that a sniper and his observer could remove each one early on at the start of the attack, when the first wave went forward. Barbed wire should have been dealt with by Bangalore torpedoes early on the first morning, to make sure there were sufficient gaps to prevent bunching up.

Local commanders should have been given targets relative to the overall plan, then told to get on and devise a solution suited to the local conditions. Constructing a new trench halfway between the front lines into no man's land did give greater security and speed up the attack.

CHAPTER NINE

Laying on a smoke-screen to hide the advancing troops and bombarding the German trench system to keep enemy heads down and inflict damage were helpful and did reduce casualties. However, greater use of counter-battery work should have been practised.

Even if the two Divisions had met up, the redoubt was too strong for the numbers used and the inability to keep the forward troops supplied with ammunition and grenades was lamentable. Rawlinson should have been less worried about his Territorials and more concerned about the gunners, re-establishing the riflemen's role as sharp-shooters.

SOURCES

An almost complete history of the Regiment is told within the pages of *The Kensingtons,* published by the Regimental Old Comrades Association. Unfortunately there are far too few names mentioned of senior non-commissioned officers. Richard Van Emden has written a series of books about the war and times, including many personal accounts. I thank sincerely the Family and Children's Services of Chelsea and Kensington Library for their continuing assistance. Much assistance has been gained from various websites, in particular British Isles Genealogy/Fifth Leicestershire Battalion, 7th Robin Hood Battalion: The Sherwood Foresters. Finally, the map has been reworked from the official 1916 edition to include later battle plans.

BIBLIOGRAPHY AND RECOMMENDED READING

The Somme, by General Sir Anthony Farrar-Hockley, Pan Grand Strategy Books 1983, chapter 3

History of The First World War, by Liddell Hart, Pan Books, 4th printing, 1976, Chapter 6

The Kensingtons, 13th London Regiment, by Sergeants Bailey and Hollier, published by the Regimental Old Comrades Association. Chapter 9, The Somme, pages 80-100.

SOURCES

The First Day on the Somme, by Martin Middlebrook. Allen Lane, 1971/Fontana 1975

Battle of the Somme, by Sir Douglas Haig's Command to the 1st July, Volume 1, London: Macmillan, 1932/Shearer Publications, 1986.

Trench Fever by Christopher Moore published by Abacus 1999: Chapter 5 Gommecourt, p 87-129. Gives a fine view of the battle on the North Midland front and an excellent account of the attack from the viewpoint of the 46th Division and in particular the part played by the Fifth Leicesters.

The Face of Battle, by John Keegan, published by Pimlico 1976, Chapter 4

Johnny Get Your Gun, by John F Tucker

Years of Combat by Lord Douglas of Kirtleside, published by The Quality Book Club 1963

Fields of Death by Peter Slowe & Richard Woods, published by Robert Hale Limited, 1986

Battle of the Somme 1916, Ten Days to Live or Die in No Man's Land, 1-14 July 1916.

The Great Push, by P Macgill

SOURCES

The Old Front Line, by John Masefield

A Lack of Offensive Spirit, by Alan MacDonald, Iona Books, 2008

World War One, by Philip Warner

The People and the British Economy, 1830-1914, by Roderick Floud

Official History of the War, Military Operations: France and Belgium 1916, Vo 1

The Private Papers of Douglas Haig, 1914-1919, ed. Robert Blake, London, 1952

Presentation Paper by Brigadier Fraser Scott MA to Royal Artillery Historical Society 22.01.2003 subject: Artillery Survey in World War One.

www.ingramcontent.com/pod-product-compliance
Lightning Source LLC
Chambersburg PA
CBHW032010040426
42448CB00006B/560